Learning by Doing

Home & School Activities for All Children

Anne Rogovin

Abingdon Press
NASHVILLE

LEARNING BY DOING:
HOME & SCHOOL ACTIVITIES FOR ALL CHILDREN

Copyright © 1998 by Anne Rogovin

All rights reserved.

This book is printed on acid-free paper.

Library of Congress Cataloging-in-Publication Data

Rogovin, Anne.
   Learning by doing : Home & School Activities for All
      Children / Anne Rogovin.
   p. cm.
   ISBN 0-687-000858 (alk. paper)
   1. Activity programs in education. 2. Creative activities and
seat work. I. Title.
371.39–dc21   98-12732
                                                   CIP

98 99 00 01 02 03 04 05 06 07–10 9 8 7 6 5 4 3 2 1

MANUFACTURED IN THE UNITED STATES OF AMERICA

T O

my mother who taught me something of compassion

my husband, MILTON

my children
ELLEN
MARK
PAULA

my grandchildren
DAVID
STEVEN
ERIC
MALAIKA
ALIYA

My great grandchild
HOSHEA

and all the beautiful children of the world

A Special Thanks
to

ROBERT COLES
Professor of Psychiatry and
Medical Humanities at Harvard

STEPHEN JAY GOULD
Alexander Agassiz Professor of Zoology at Harvard

*who believe in my work and took their valuable
time to evaluate and write for my book.*

CONTENTS

FOREWORD

This wonderfully accessible, knowing, helpful book will bring much joy to many teachers and students—a gift of love from a teacher who has had a lot of experience working with those "who learn slowly." Anne Rogovin brings to her fellow teachers, and to the students, a writer's straightness of expression, an artist's visual imagination, and a longtime educator's directness of manner or approach. From the title on she makes clear her intention: to help other classrooms with a series of ideas, suggestions, tips, plans for study, for action. Her recommendations are so obviously useful; are at times inspired; and are, in their sum, a gesture of generosity which will, I am sure, be much appreciated by countless teachers and their students across the land.

As I read this book, I thought of two great American educational philosophers of the past, the great psychologist William James and the great social essayist John Dewey, each of whom worried hard and long about America's schools—their nature and purposes. James was a pragmatist—he wanted us to emphasize the practical, the useful as we teach our children at home and at school. Dewey believed in encouraging the young to connect directly with the world around them, to master that world by paying careful attention to it, by learning how things work—in the very words of this book's title, "learning by doing." Both those brilliant men of letters, those wise psychological observers, those discerning and able teachers, would be ever so delighted, surely, by this effort of a late-twentieth-century idealist who has spent her life giving of herself, mind, heart, and soul, to any number of vulnerable and needy students, whose struggles she has made her own, and whose special challenges and needs she understands, and wants others also to understand.

Here, then, are charts and drawings and songs, brief and lucid essays, all sorts of recommendations—here, certainly, is a series of well-conceived, well-articulated "lessons," aimed at those who teach and those who need to learn, but so doing, require the attentive patience and concern of the men and women who are their classroom instructors. But these pages amount to something else, as well—they will be a companion of sorts to many, the young and those who aim to help the young grow intellectually, emotionally, morally: a source of good cheer, of thoughtful, sensitively stated plans with which a class can be encouraged to work together, think together, learn together. For such a contribution to our nation's children who will find their way to the pages that follow, all of us owe Anne Rogovin a great round of enthusiastic applause; she is a person of great dedication, enormous moral energy, high and solid and sensible intelligence, who has devoted a big part of her life to working with the kind of young people who will be using this book—and for such a commitment, lived out intensely over all these past years, she deserves to be held in our highest esteem and regard, honored with all the devotion we as her fellow citizens, her fellow teachers, can manage to muster. If this book is her great contribution to many of our teachers, our children, their reciprocal gift to its author, a precious one, certainly, will be (one hopes) its constant use in school after school of our nation.

—Robert Coles

PREFACE

Again and again, our corporate and highly technological society falls into a fundamental error in trying to understand both the causes of breakthroughs and the basis of continuing effectiveness. If advanced machinery and power lunches drive our culture (wherever it might be headed), then any difficult problem may best be solved by a technological fix dictated by large corporate boards or research teams. I cannot imagine any deeper or more serious mistake in our understanding of human creativity and social change.

One wise, compassionate, committed, and experienced person, with good access to sage advice, but unfettered in freedom to judge, can do more (and better) than the biggest bureaucracy with the shiniest and most expensive tools. The history of science has continually shown this power of small resources (used by maximally expansive minds)—from Galileo with his telescope to Darwin in his library. The human brain, after all, remains the most powerful and complex of all machines. And the moral and intellectual force of one good person—free to think, to judge, to seek advice, and to act—can move mountains.

We are enmeshed, we are told, in a crisis in education. In particular, so-called special education for students with mental retardation (or whatever the language police now favors as a euphemism) is said to be commandeering a gluttonous share of the resources and bankrupting the system—for we need fancy tests, elaborate rooms, expensive equipment, and endless specialist fees; costs therefore skyrocket beyond the power of local school boards to cope.

As the father of an autistic son, I support with all my heart and moral sense the proposition that we must struggle unceasingly—with whatever time and money required—to give our citizens with impairments as much intellectual, practical, and ethical education as can possibly be beneficial. Going further, I would say that the moral worth of a society may be judged by a willingness to bear the extra effort and expense that such projects require. What I do not accept, however, is the high-tech corporate model of pursuit—throw more money, fancier equipment, and ever larger conferences of theorists at the problem, and best solutions will emerge.

Give me one great and experienced teacher any time, a person who has devoted the best years of her life to the combination of deep thought, unquestioned commitment, and practical experience that defines success in this hardest and most important of all professions. (I have often said that "teacher" must be the noblest word in our language. I might have nominated "parent," except that, after a certain point, parents have no choice, while teachers must pursue their calling voluntarily.) Anne Rogovin is the prototype of such a wise and heroic teacher. For half a century, she has learned what works with slow learners and students with mental impairments by learning with them, improving from their successes, and constantly refining her methods by the ultimate test of experience.

Above all, she has discovered that these students, like all students at all levels, do best by active engagement—by trying and doing, more than by listening or taking formal tests. Moreover, and most important, she finds that you don't need fancy special equipment, manufactured in small quantities at great cost just for the occasion. The humblest and most ordinary objects of nature and human manufacture—the items found in every kitchen, on every city street, on every field and pond—can inspire questions, provoke experiments, provide joy and puzzlement, and slake curiosity, as well as the expensive high-tech razzle-dazzle of buttons and flashing lights in our "advanced" interactive classrooms and museums. We should even prefer the humble and equally instructive objects because they are inexpensive and ready to hand—part of the familiar world so important for all people, especially those with mental impairments.

I parlayed my own childhood fascination for nature into a career as a paleontologist and taxonomist. I suppose I could have learned about the science of classification from expensive microscope sets (but my family didn't have the funds), or complex and ingenious programs at museum computer terminals (but they didn't exist in my youth). Instead, I trace my love for, and my learning about, organic diversity to the two earliest devices that I can remember using. My grandmother used to take me to the only neighborhood spot of green in our section of New York City—a triangular plot of grass called McDonald Park and located between two diagonally converging streets. She would bring a cigar box and some sticks to serve as dividers. I would then classify and collect nature in the park, putting different items into the sections of my box—grass in one, leaves in another, dirt in a third, pebbles in a fourth. My father often took me to Rockaway Beach, where I loved to collect shells. I placed them in the three bags we always brought along—labeled, by my instructions, with the three categories I had chosen for ordering my limited world: ordinary, unusual, and extraordinary. I plunged in and learned with all the thrill and benefit of a team of physicists in their particle accelerator.

—*Stephen Jay Gould*

If I Could

If I could I would give you the flower
that brightens your day
I would give you the rain that waters the earth,
and the trees that shade the forest.

If I could I would give you the moon that
shines at night. I would give you the stars that
fill the sky, and the sun that shines so bright.

If I could I would give you the birds'
songs that wake you up each morning. I would
give you the shells from the sea, and the
sand from the beach.

If I could.

—*Aliya Hart*

LeTTeR To MY ReADeRS

Dear Parents and Teachers:

This book was written for those thousands (perhaps millions) of children who can learn, but who learn slowly and learn best by DOING.

They may be children who are considered:

>average or "normal"
>mentally retarded
>autistic (those children who have little aware-
>   ness of themselves or their surroundings)
>learning disabled
>emotionally disturbed
>orthopedically impaired
>multiply handicapped
>speech, hearing, or visually impaired

They may be children who can be found anywhere. They can be:

>your sister or your brother
>your neighbor
>on the block where you live
>in your neighborhood
>in every city
>   and
>every country around the world

They are children who can be found among:

>the rich and the poor
>all races
>all colors
>   and
>all creeds

These are children who, like ALL CHILDREN, can:

>laugh
>cry
>hate
>fear
>   and
>love

My thirty years of teaching have taught me that children do best when activities or materials are IMPORTANT and RELEVANT to their lives *now*—and not because they are told "Do it because it's good for you!"

My years of teaching have taught me that a child sitting quietly at a desk or sitting passively before a television set or a computer is *not* learning as well as the child actively involved—in activities and with materials that can be EXPERIENCED, HANDLED, FELT, and become a part (however small) of the child's life. Children must be allowed to experience

> delights
> triumphs
> making choices
> imagining
> hearing, smelling, tasting
> exploring,
> observing

In all this, a child thinks . . .

> If you want me to learn . . .
> please don't hurry me . . .
>
> Let me play around with the things
> you have for me . . .
>
> Let me find out things for myself . . .
> I just know I can find out lots of . . .
>
> . . . in time . . .
> . . . if you don't hurry me . . .
>
> PLEASE . . .

Take whatever you will from my book. If you can get even *one* worthwhile idea that would make the child's life more productive and a little happier—please know that all my efforts will be justified and will make me feel "good inside."

Sincerely,

Anne Rogovin

INTRODUCTION

"Everyone calls me dummy . . . seems like I can't do nuthin' right."

Johnny's memory is short.
It is hard for him to pay attention and concentrate on facts and
  details.
He can't understand the abstract.

"Yes'm . . . yes'm."

Johnny has failed so many times before, he doesn't want to fail again.

"Naw . . . I don't wanna play."

Learning has meant only a cowed acceptance.
He becomes adept at looking pleased and interested when he is
  being talked to, though his mind is likely vacant. He may be glad
  not to have to make a mental effort.
Johnny rarely gets into trouble.
You wish he would show more spunk.
He even seems unwilling or unable to look around.

The philosophy of every parent or teacher must be an abiding faith in
the basic worth of *all* human beings. The very differences that are
observed in the child must be the foundation of all the parents' or
teachers' efforts.

Parents and teachers must guide the child out of the problems which
disturb and defeat the child into a positive acceptance of the child's
worth and the child's willingness to "go along."

SCIENCE

1. SCIENCE

"I just can't find time to have anything to do with nature." One hears this so often and it's somewhat disappointing. I deeply feel (especially in these days of speed, synthetics, and materialism) that being close to living things—seeing their beauty and wonder, and the priceless good feelings they can give us—makes a love of nature very important for everyone.

A love of nature doesn't necessarily mean the technical study of it, with technical names and definitions to memorize. Instead, it means encouraging a child's fancies—

> the light
> the moon
> the rain
> the wind
> a falling star
> a seedpod found on the walk
> the storm clouds that blacken the sky
> a robin on the lawn
> the maple syrup on the breakfast pancakes
> or an ant carrying a breadcrumb.

Let us take children and lead them to the precious wonders of the earth and sky.

SCIENCE animal pets

Encourage children to observe. (I have found that the good habit of observation can persist for a lifetime, even though the specific subject matter is long forgotten.) When they are ready, encourage them to record their observations. Observing a pet mouse is a fun way to begin.

Notes about Squeeky

Jan. 6 — Squeeky has a real long tail. He climbs with it.

Jan. 7 — Squeeky fell off the table. He got lost. He runs fast.

Jan. 12 — 7 babies got born. They are pink.
1 2 3 4 5 6 7
They do not have any hair on.

17

Having guinea pigs as pets can mean more than just fun. It means these funny little animals can help a child to develop a sense of responsibility: for guinea pigs need to be fed, their water changed daily, and their cages cleaned. (Besides developing a child's sense of responsibility, think of what a wonderful lesson in "life" it could be if you have a male and a female pig!)

SCIENCE fish

If a child can experience looking at a fish—perhaps a fish in its home fish tank, perhaps at a fish store or supermarket, the child will find out that A FISH HAS SEVEN FINS. Try it!

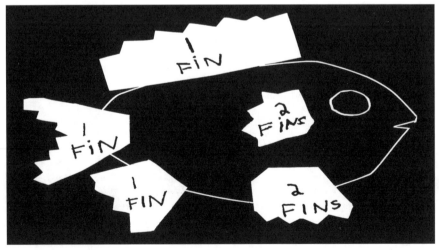

To watch more than a dozen guppies emerging from the mother "live" and able to swim away "on their own" is a marvelous phenomenon for anyone to behold! In another tank, watch the tropical fish born from a cluster of tiny eggs.

If you're lucky enough to be near a pond or stream, why not catch some fish? "Uncultured" fish are just as exciting as "cultured" ones. Put them in a pail of water. Be sure to change the water every day. Watch them for a few days, then please—oh please—be sure to return them to the pond. (You can easily exchange them for some others another time!)

SCIENCE plants

Do you know the parts of a flower? Look at a flower. See the petals, the leaves, and the stem.

Can you make a flower and write in the names of the parts? Of course, you can!

Some girls and some boys have a special flair for making attractive flower arrangements. What fun it is to make centerpieces for family get-togethers, social functions like parties or meetings, or just to look at for enjoyment.

You never know. Perhaps with lots of practice a child might become a florist's helper!

SCIENCE plant notebook

Leaves are all around. A LEAF NOTEBOOK helps build an awareness of their different shapes and fall colors. If the details are brought to children's attention, they can study the veins and see how the leaves are fed.

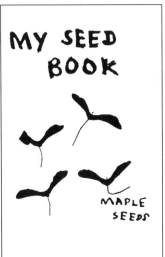

SCIENCE wildflowers

A nearby vacant lot is made-to-order for finding some of the most spectacular treasures of the world:

> the dandelion's feathery head with its seeds sailing off in the wind
> brilliant yellow buttercups waiting to be placed under chins for the
>   "if you like butter" test
> the delightful design of Queen Anne's lace
> jack-in-the-pulpit
> the oozing white sap of the milkweed
> black-eyed Susans
> sweet clover (See if you can find a 4-leaf clover!)
> prickly thistle

When the days get shorter and the cold begins to freeze our fingers:

> we watch the whirling red, yellow, and purple leaves dance to the
>   ground.
> we pick the white-oak acorns and horse chestnuts.
> we look for winter buds, the tiny beginnings of next year's twigs and
>   leaves.

If you get an unused clothes hanger and suspend some leaves from it, you have a leaf mobile. Hang it up (especially where it can get a breeze) and see how everyone will enjoy it.

Try making necklaces from colored corn seeds. Apple seeds also make handsome necklaces.

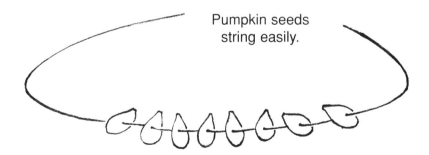

Pumpkin seeds string easily.

(Friends and relatives will enjoy saving seeds for these two projects.)

SCIENCE bird projects

You can feed the birds in the winter by placing suet or peanut butter on pinecones.

It seems that in the hurried society we have nowadays, few are very interested in birds. It is so sad that there is so little interest in our feathered friends, for an awareness of them can bring so much added beauty and joy into our lives. Since birds are all around us, wherever we go, no money or special effort is required. We can see them on our way to school or the corner store while we sit on our porchsteps looking out a bus window.

Some even remain in the winter for us to feed and enjoy.

It's thrilling with binoculars to be able to "come close" to a bird.

If we don't take birds for granted but learn to "pay attention," we can marvel at the exquisite feathers of a turkey or a chicken. How exciting it is to look up for a moment and watch a bird in flight, or to listen to the robin's or chickadee's cheery song.

Orioles build their nests as pockets, which dangle from a limb. Do they do this to get a "free ride" when the breezes blow?

It is deeply moving to see a flock of migrating birds
     a mother sparrow teaching its young to fly
     a robin scratching for worms in the damp earth.

Such are the "little things" that wait only for one's eyes to be opened wider.

SCIENCE visits to make

There are so many exciting things in the country that you can't see in the city.

I have often wished people could spend some time living in the country, on a farm, away from the hurried, sophisticated demands of urban living. Since it isn't always possible, what can we do? We can read about the farm or watch movies or television programs about farms, but none of this is enough. Sooner or later, we must have firsthand experiences with the farm. We must take a trip!

We must:
- smell the hay in the barn.
- stroke the sheep's wool.
- watch the herd of cows chewing their cuds in the shade and see how they are milked.
- listen to the constant grunting of pigs in the sty.
- listen to the hen clucking when she leads her chicks so that they know where she is in the tall grass.
- ride in the farmer's horse-drawn wagon down the country road.
- hear chicks peeping
  - the rooster crowing
  - owls hooting
  - tree frogs peeping.
- see a gently flowing stream
  - a cherry orchard
  - a field of clover.
- see how wheat from which our bread is made grows
  - a family of ducks.
- taste a delicious apple right from the apple tree.

Other exciting places to visit someday could be
- a fish hatchery
- a flower market
- a quarry where fossils can be collected
- a lumberyard
- a dog kennel
- a cheese factory
  - or
- a nearby waterfall
- a burnt-out forest
- a restored village
- a maple syrup farm
- a fish cannery

Did you ever make a "picture story"? Do you know that sometimes a picture story is lots of fun to make? Besides, a picture story can help you remember and understand something more easily than a straightforward description.

Picture stories aren't hard to make up. Any grown-up can make one up. Or, better yet—why can't the children make one up? A grown-up can help, if necessary.

Try this technique to help explain rain, clouds, snow, and frost.

A Story That Doesn't End

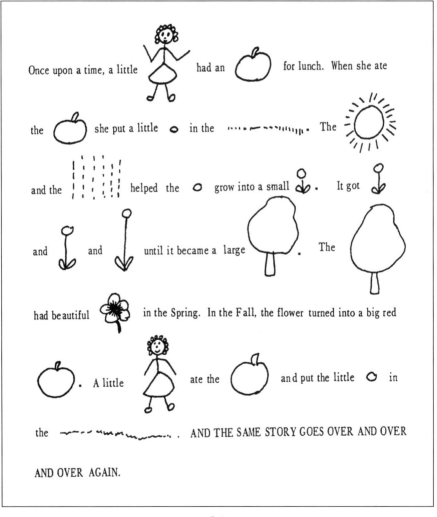

Once upon a time, a little [girl] had an [apple] for lunch. When she ate the [apple] she put a little [seed] in the [ground]. The [sun] and the [rain] helped the [seed] grow into a small [sprout]. It got [bigger] and [bigger] and [bigger] until it became a large [tree]. The [tree] had beautiful [blossoms] in the Spring. In the Fall, the flower turned into a big red [apple]. A little [girl] ate the [apple] and put the little [seed] in the ground. AND THE SAME STORY GOES OVER AND OVER AND OVER AGAIN.

24

HEALTH

2. HEALTH

Some form of health training should be a part of a child's life every single day.

HEALTH inspection

Some children don't know how to take a bath or shower properly. A daily "check-off" list helps to make children conscious of their personal health habits. Sometimes when the list is a large "public" or "family" one, children become more aware of others' deficiencies and "get after" the errant person to make improvements. (Sometimes criticism from peers or other family members can be more effective than a nagging parent or a teacher.)

HEALTH care of teeth

Getting dentist or dental hygienist reports on some children can be painful. Some have so many teeth problems. It may well be that some children inherit tendencies for poor dental health, but some of the problems stem from outright neglect. First sets of teeth may not be taken seriously and not given the important care so vitally needed. Crooked teeth may not be straightened when they should be. Teeth are extracted in some instances when perhaps they could have been saved. Candy, pop, and pastries are consumed with little restraint, and (afterward) the teeth are not brushed or are poorly brushed.

It is up to us, as adults, to instill good health habits as early as possible—at home, at school, and wherever the child might be.

Repetition is something most children thrive on.
  After eating breakfast, lunch, or dinner, does the child brush teeth?
  Does the child brush teeth after a snack like juice or an apple?
  After a party, does the child brush teeth?

This adds up to a lot of time just for the teeth. But if the time spent NOW helps in any way to establish the habit of better dental care, the time is well spent.

HEALTH care of eyes

"You see, the eye is like a camera," says a visiting optometrist.

  How do you get something out of your eye?
  Can too much sun hurt your eyes?
  What is the best way to set your glasses down when you are not wearing them?
  Can watching too much television harm your eyes?
  What do you think of contact lenses?
  Why is it important to have regular eye examinations? to wear your glasses regularly? to clean your glasses?
  What are the dangers of a snowball fight?
  Can eye makeup cause problems?

28

These are the kinds of questions that come up from time to time. An adult may be able to answer some or all of these questions, but not as convincingly as the visiting optometrist who is trained specifically in eye care. I believe that children can sense this authority and (hopefully) gain a healthier respect for their eyes as one of their most precious possessions.

There are many optometrists or opticians who would be more than happy to be invited to discuss the eye—or would be happy to answer a child's questions.

HEALTH posture

How much more meaningful talking about "good posture" becomes when children can actually see a skeleton. Bones are no longer just "something hard" underneath the skin. Matters such as exercise, food digestion, cigarette smoking, good posture, the need for sex education—become more meaningful to children when they can be related to a three-dimensional body.

HEALTH care of hair

The visit of a nearby beautician or a visit to a nearby beauty salon is "just right" for some children. Familiar with all the latest hair styles, the professional beautician communicates easily with children (sometimes even better than parents or children's teacher!). At the same time too, the children are impressed with some basic information on hair care:

How to wash one's hair and how often, and what to use for shampooing
How to comb and brush hair properly
The "do's" and "don'ts" of using other people's combs, brushes, etc.

HEALTH care of nails

No parent or teacher can be expected to solve the problem of nail-biting easily. It is often thought that nail-biting may be an outward manifestation of a more serious, more deeply rooted problem. Yet, when the professional manicurist encourages a child with such remarks as, "How nice you will look if you let your nails grow . . ." and the child begins to feel good about herself, we have moved toward alleviating the problem.

29

HEALTH shaving

Why not buy an electric razor and have the child's "own" shaver easily available for when there is just the right amount of "fuzz." Why not make this little period an important occasion—just as we talk about all the wonderful, remarkable changes that take place in the bodies of all children at the teenage period!

HEALTH smoking

Many children are gullible and some may take or want to take up smoking. They see their parents and other role models smoking. Newspaper ads and billboards extol the enjoyment of smoking. Smoking is often "in" with their peers. In casual samplings of groups of teenagers, one invariably finds some who already smoke and several who will be smoking soon.

It is very difficult to counteract the continuous promotion of smoking, but that doesn't mean adults should give up trying all kinds of techniques. For example, once we invited for a visit a doctor from a nearby cancer clinic. He discussed the dangers of smoking and then supplemented this with a film and slides. Some of the scenes of the organs destroyed by smoking are horrible! But if these slides in any way deter one student from smoking—then we can be thankful!

HEALTH first aid

No matter where a person may be, there is always the element of danger and possibility of an accident. This is why a basic knowledge of first aid is vital for children.

A phone call to a Red Cross group is often all that is needed to provide a class in first aid. There are many classes in first aid students can attend. Red Cross workers are glad to share their knowledge and also provide the necessary practice in such techniques as:

    How to make a sling
    Bandages for a head injury or a knee injury
    What to do for burns
    How to take care of cuts and bruises
    How to stop a nosebleed
    How to make simple bandages

Care of burns (including sunburn)
How to move an injured person
What to do for dog, insect, and snake bites
How to treat a headache, earache, or toothache
Identification and treatment for poison ivy
What to do if a person faints
How to call for a doctor
What to include in a first-aid kit.

HEALTH street safety

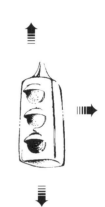

In our sprawling, bustling cities, with thousands of cars, getting from place to place is not an easy job for anyone. Yet, children must get about. They must get to school, to their jobs, to the stores, and so forth. To learn about safety rules, why not practice by making up little plays. For example, a play on how to:

cross at corners, with and without a signal
cross quickly and not loiter on the street
get in and out of a bus or car
walk on the road, if one must.

As worthwhile as it is to practice safety rules indoors, eventually children must face the reality of the street. This is often a trying time for

the adult because there are many elements of danger involved. A good solution that can sometimes be worked out is to discuss the problem with the nearby police station personnel. Sometimes they can assign a police officer to work with the children for a short time each day for a week. This can be very helpful, since the police officer can control the traffic as the children practice, and his or her presence gives the children the added confidence they need. After a week, try practice without the police officer—with only the teacher or parent. After another week or so, children can be given the opportunity to practice alone.

HEALTH bicycle safety

So many children on bicycles—young and old—are allured to the street. If they would limit their riding to safe areas, we adults would have no grave fears. But they do not. We talk about the dangers, but they often go to the streets in spite of our warnings. The most we can do is to give children heavy doses of safety lessons.

A most valuable resource is the personable worker at the bicycle shop. He knows how to communicate with young people (not all people can do this well!). In his casual, easygoing manner, he covers a great deal of important material convincingly. The children seem to say to themselves, "Gosh, this guy really knows what he's talking about. . . . I'll believe him."

The children are shown the parts that need to be lubricated regularly, the parts that need tightening and how to do it, how to check the air in tires, how to adjust the brakes and the seat, and so forth. He also discusses the importance of using the bell or horn, the reflectors for night-riding, keeping away from open car doors, and how to carry packages on the bicycle.

HEALTH home nursing

With some Red Cross groups you can borrow a whole truckload of home nursing equipment. Here is a list of some of the equipment we once received:

> 2 blankets (one light and one heavy)
> 2 sheets, 2 pillows, and 2 pillowcases
> 6 thermometers
> 2 basins and soap for washing
> 1 hot water bag and 3 ice packs
> a set of plastic dishes (including plastic flowers!)
> a folding bed and mattress

Not pressing to return the materials quickly (the Red Cross had said, "Keep them as long as you need them . . . when you're through, just give us a call and we will pick them up"), we covered the following material:

> how to feed and bathe a sick patient
> how to make a bed and care for the bedroom
> how to read thermometers, use ice packs and hot water bags
> how to make a patient comfortable, to change positions, to
>   relieve pressure, to keep the room quiet, etc.

There is presently a shortage of nurses and nurses' aides for hospitals and nursing homes. This training may encourage a student to go into this field someday.

HEALTH physical education

Physical education is an area where children who may not do well in academics can often excel. These children can often run well, hit a baseball well, or do handsprings well. In the gymnasium or at a park, very often the poorer academic student can find a new identity.

It seems that most children love physical education activities and participate quite fully. A program of physical education could consist of:

GROUP GAMES	OUTDOOR SPORTS	STUNTS
bowling	swimming	trampoline
shuffleboard	rowing	handsprings
table tennis	fishing	rope climbing
baseball	hiking	chinning
dodgeball	roller skating	somersaults

Any physical education person dealing with children has the important responsibility to:

1) Make directions *simple, repeat* directions, and *demonstrate directions.*
2) Realize that some children lack spontaneity and have to be encouraged to participate. (But—once they get involved in a group— these same children usually want to play as long as they can!)

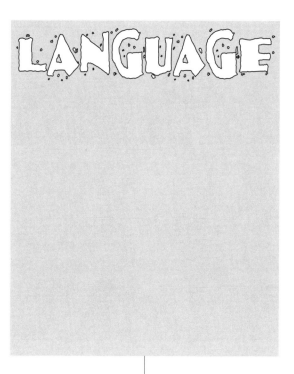

G

3. LANGUAGE

CHORAL SPEECHES give precious opportunities for oral language to develop and to make sure the children have fun learning how. When I was younger, I was petrified if asked to speak before a group of people. Then, after a while—with more speaking experience—speaking before groups became easier. And so it usually is with children.

It is interesting sometimes to watch a child who may be bashful when participating in a choral speech. This same child

    may just sit for days without opening her mouth.
    Sometimes she will just look around at the others.
    More days will pass—
    and then, one fine day her lips will begin moving.

A week or so later, you will hear this same girl participating with the words of the speech! And then that great day comes when our once bashful youngster is performing eagerly with the rest of the children. A real victory!

It is also interesting to watch an aggressive youngster, with perhaps a boisterous voice and rough-house ways. The child may upset the group for a while. Then somehow, subtle pressures from the group change this child into a cooperative human being. It's as if the child begins to realize that the success of the performance depends on his or her cooperation.

The following traditional poems, songs, and stories can be broken up into different parts with one, two, three, or more children having separate parts. Also there are parts where all the children can speak together.

Break them up any way you wish and with as many parts as you wish. Try them and enjoy! Some of these choral speeches are just plain silly, but some can incidentally "teach important lessons"!

If you want added fun, why not try using gestures or acting out some of the parts.

TWO FROGS

Two frogs fell into a milk pail deep,
    Croak, croak, croak!
And one poor frog did nothing but weep,
    Croak, croak, croak!
He sank to the bottom as heavy as lead,
    Croak, croak, croak!
And there in the morning they found him dead,
    Croak, croak, croak!
The other frog shouted, "I'll have a good try."
    Croak, croak, croak!
"The pail may be deep, but I don't want to die."
    Croak, croak, croak!
He churned up the milk with his legs fore and hind,
    Croak, croak, croak!
There's nothing like having a masterful mind,
    Croak, croak, croak!
For when the next morning this froggy was found,
    Croak, croak, croak!
A fresh pat of butter he floated around,
    Croak, croak, croak!

JEFF BROWN

Jeff Brown was riding up Shuter's bank.
   He-haw, he-haw, he-haw!

The old gray mule did kick and prank,
   He-haw, he-haw, he-haw!

Jeff Brown was riding up Shuter's hill.
   He-haw, he-haw, he-haw!

His mule fell down, Jeff took a spill.
   He-haw, he-haw, he-haw!

The bridle and saddle are now on the shelf,
   He-haw, he-haw, he-haw!

If you want any more you can sing it yourself.
   He-haw, he-haw, he-haw!

JUST LIKE ME (Mother Goose)

"I went up one pair of stairs."
   "Just like me." *(Child repeats this line.)*
"I went up two pair of stairs."
   "Just like me."
"I looked out of the window."
   "Just like me."
"And there I saw a monkey."
   "Just like me."

BUZZ, HMMM

"Buzz," says the blue fly.
"Hmmm," says the bee.
"Buzz," and "Hmmm," they cry,
And so do we.

Buzz, Hmmm! Buzz, Hmmm!
Buzz, Hmmm, Buzz!

THE NORTH WIND

The north wind blew.
It rattled the windows.
It swept down the flue.
The great trees groaned.

Owwwwwwwww! Owwwwwwwww!
Owwwwwwwww!

OLD JACK FROST

Who sweetens up the summer fruit?
   Old Jack Frost!
Who gives the tree his new fall suit?
   Old Jack Frost!
Who brings the walnut tumbling down?
Who makes the chestnut sweet and brown?
Who yellows up the pumpkin's gown?
   Old Jack Frost!
What bites the little children's toes?
   Old Jack Frost!
Who causes white all out of doors?
   Old Jack Frost!
Who makes your bones creep?
Who makes you crawl up a heap?
And call for covers when you sleep?
   Old Jack Frost!

IF YOU'RE HAPPY AND YOU KNOW IT

(Suit action to the words.)

> If you're happy and you know it, clap your hands.
> If you're happy and you know it, clap your hands.
> If you're happy and you know it,
> Then your face will surely show it,
> If you're happy and you know it, clap your hands.
>
> If you're sad and you know it, wipe your eyes.
> If you're sad and you know it, wipe your eyes.
> If you're sad and you know it,
> Then your face will surely show it,
> If you're sad and you know it, wipe your eyes.
>
> If you're mad and you know it, stamp your feet, etc.

(Repeat first verse.)

Libraries usually have lots of books with choral speeches. Look them up sometime. Children LOVE them.

LANGUAGE finger plays

Children from generation to generation have always enjoyed FINGER PLAYS.

Finger plays give delightful opportunities to communicate thoughts and feelings. They provide opportunities to communicate— through the use of words, gestures, animal sounds, and so on.

The main thing to remember about finger plays is that *there are no rules to follow.*

   If a finger wants to wiggle or slither— that's OK.
   If a finger wants to croak like a bullfrog or purr like a cat, that's OK too.

There are loads of books on finger plays that can be obtained at libraries. Better yet, why not have children make up some! In the meantime try some of these that younger children love:

I HAVE TEN LITTLE FINGERS

(Suit actions to words.)

> I have ten little fingers
> And they all belong to me.
> I can shut them up tight
> Or open them wide.
> I can put them together
> Or make them all hide.
> I can make them jump high,
> I can make them jump low,
> I can fold them quietly,
> And hold them just so.

BABY SEEDS

In a milkweed cradle   *(Form cradle with both hands.)*
Snug and warm.
Baby seeds are hiding
Safe from harm.
Open wide the cradle   *(Open hands.)*
Hold it high   *(Hold hands up high.)*
Come, Mr. Wind.
Help them fly.   *(Wave hands above head.)*

THE APPLE TREE

Way up high in the apple tree,   *(Reach high with hand.)*
Two round apples smiled at me   *(Point to self.)*
I shook that tree as hard as I could   *(Shake hands.)*
And down came the apples   *(Let hands fall.)*
Mmmmmmmm, mmmmmm they were good.   *(Rub belly.)*

DRAW A CIRCLE

Draw a circle, draw a circle　　　　　*(Draw a circle in air.)*
Round as can be,
Draw a circle, draw a circle
Just for me.　　　　　　　　　　　　*(Point to self.)*

Draw a square, draw a square　　　　*(Draw a square in air.)*
Square as can be,
Draw a square, draw a square
Just for me.　　　　　　　　　　　　*(Point to self.)*

Draw a triangle, draw a triangle　　*(Draw a triangle in air.)*
With corners three,
Draw a triangle, draw a triangle
Just for me.　　　　　　　　　　　　*(Point to self.)*

TWO EYES TO SEE

Two lips to smile the whole day through,　　*(Point to each body part*
Two eyes to see nice things to do,　　　　　*as it is mentioned.)*
Two hands to put the toys away,
A tongue to speak kind words each day,
Two feet that errands quickly run,
Make happy times for everyone.

I STRETCH MY FINGERS

I stretch my fingers away up high　　*(Suit actions to words.)*
Until they almost reach the sky,
I lay them in my lap, you see,　　　　*(Touch body parts as mentioned.)*
Where they're as quiet as can be!

CLAP YOUR HANDS

Clap your hands, clap your hands, *(Point to each body part*
Clap them just like me. *as it is mentioned.)*
Touch your shoulders, touch your shoulders,
Touch them just like me.
Shake your head, shake your head,
Shake it just like me.
Clap your hands, clap your hands,
Now let them quiet be. *(Fold hands in lap.)*

THE TOUCH GAME

Touch your nose, *(Touch body parts as*
Touch your chin, *each is mentioned.)*
That's the way this game begins.
Touch your eyes,
Touch your knees, *(Suit actions to words.)*
Now pretend you're going to sneeze.
Touch your hair,
Touch your ear,
Touch your two lips right here.
Touch your elbows
Where they bend.
That's the way this touch game ends.

STAND UP TALL

Stand up tall; *(Suit actions to words.)*
Hands in the air;
Clap your hands;
Make a frown;
Smile and smile;
And flop like a clown!

MUSIC AT OUR HOUSE

Mother plays the violin,   *(Suit actions to words.)*
Father plays the flute,
Little brother plays the horn—
Toot-toot-toot-toot-toot.

SHHH!

Shhh . . . be very quiet.   *(Suit actions to words.)*
Shhh . . . be very still.
Fold your busy, busy hands.
Close your sleepy, sleepy eyes.
Shhh . . . be very still.

NOW I AM A SNOWMAN

Now I am a snowman   *(Stand with arms out.)*
Standing on the lawn.
I melt and melt and melt   *(Body slumps and voice
                                                         fades.)*

And pretty soon I'm gone.

RAIN IS FALLING DOWN

Rain is falling down, rain is falling down   *(Raise arms, flutter
Pitter-patter, pitter-patter   fingers to ground.)*
Rain is falling down.

47

LANGUAGE puppetry

Here are some puppet "shows" you might care to begin with. I am sure you can think of lots of others.

A scene at the breakfast table gives children practice in table manners. The children may decide to chop off the head of anyone who forgets the appropriate "please." This can become a bit gory, but then again—it's fun to cut off the head of a puppet once in a while!

A water pipe is leaking. Tom must call the plumber to come and fix it. (This could be good training in the event of emergencies—and it's also a lot of fun to do too!)

Sally refuses to go out with Jim. Why? Because he smells. He really should try to take a bath or a shower more often. Or should he use deodorant? Delicate subjects are much easier to discuss when a puppet is talking than talking directly to other people.

Emma's mother is sick. How does she telephone the doctor? Puppets will give lots of fun practice in telephoning for a doctor.

Mary is sitting on a park bench. A stranger walks up to her. He asks her to go for a ride with him. What should Mary do?

Jim is smoking a cigarette. He asks Melvin if he would like a cigarette too. What should Melvin say?

Can you think of a puppet TV show about drugs? helping others? pornography? what else?

Puppets are very accommodating. They can help children say things they would not ordinarily say and do things they would not ordinarily do.

For developing good language skills, very few techniques can be rated higher than puppetry (or puppet TV, as it can be called). When other activities cause children to yawn and wish they were outside playing, the silly awkward movements of puppets take the children out of the world of reality and hold them spellbound in a world of make-believe.

There is hardly anything that is faster (or cheaper) to make than a puppet—even a first-class puppet! Here are some you might like to try out:

A Just-Your-Finger Puppet

Just a finger can sometimes teach better than a lecture about "standing up nice and tall" or when to say "please."

A Fist Puppet	Just use your fist plain or cover it with a handkerchief (and decorate it if you want to). This is especially good for being a ghost!
A Wooden Spoon Puppet	Use a plain spoon or paint a face on it if you want to. If you need curls, twist strips of paper around it with a pencil.
A Toothpick Puppet	Just fasten a nut, grape, radish, or cherry onto a toothpick or a thin twig. (A shoebox would make just the right size stage for this one.)
A Peanut Puppet	Next time you eat peanuts, shell one carefully in half so that the shell will fit your finger. The peanut puppet can be plain or a face put on it with felt-tip marker or crayons.
Adhesive Tape Puppet	Put a piece of adhesive tape on the tip of your finger. If you put adhesive tape on your other fingers, you can have a whole family of puppets and they can talk together. Add faces if you want to.
Stick Puppet	Just draw or cut out characters from old books or magazines and attach them to a tongue depressor or ice cream stick.
Paper Bag Puppet	Cut two holes in a small, brown-paper bag. The holes are for your fingers. Add a face if you want.
Thimble Puppet	Just put a thimble or thimbles on your fingers as needed and decorate with felt-tip markers.

Puppets will perform anywhere. An "instant" stage will do very well. Anything you can get behind can become a fine stage. Here are some possibilities to try:

behind a couch

a doorway with a sheet across the bottom half

a window stage *(Attach a towel across an open window.)*

a box stage *(Cut the bottom of an old, thick carton, stand it on its side, and get into a position that screens you from view.)*

A table is tipped over on its side for a lesson on the use of the word "please":

"Mother, I'm through eating. May I please go out to play?"

The same table is covered with paper for a lesson on dating:

"C'mon, Heather—give me a kiss."

"No, Alex—I can't give you a kiss on our first date. Wait till we know each other better."

LANGUAGE pantomime

"I don't know what to say." How many times do we hear children say this? Sometimes it is quite true; a child may not know what to say in a particular situation. Sometimes it is hard for children to express thoughts in words. So, let's make it easier for these children. Let's try pantomimes. We can give children chances to do things without words. Here are some pantomimes you might care to try:

Pretend you lost your hairbrush and you're looking for it.

You're sitting on a park bench. Some pigeons come along and you are giving them some bread crumbs.

You're helping Mother clean the house. The throw rugs need shaking.

You're making toast and you accidentally burn your finger.

What do you do when you get ready for school?

While visiting a friend, you accidentally knock over her vase.

What game do you play on sidewalks? Show me how you play it.

What do you do when you see some beautiful flowers?

You're camping in the woods. How do you chop wood?

50

Another pantomime is to make believe you are someone else. This is a bit harder—but is still lots of fun (and the children do not realize that their imaginations are being stretched):

a bellhop helping with suitcases
a person washing the floor
a model with a gorgeous long gown
a farmer planting seeds
a barber giving a haircut
the gas station attendant filling the gas tank
the bus driver at the wheel
the music teacher leading a song
a policeman directing traffic

a tiger
an airplane
a truck driver
a mother or a father
a king or a queen
a bride or a bridegroom
a mail carrier delivering
    the mail

For young children, nursery rhymes lend themselves to pantomimes:

There Was a Crooked Man
Jack Be Nimble
Hey, Diddle Diddle
Humpty Dumpty
Solomon Grundy

Can you pantomime these activities?

running
skating
playing ball
throwing snowballs
swimming like a fish
shoveling snow
kicking a ball
riding a horse
crawling
flying like a bat

leaping like a kangaroo
flying like a bird
crawling like a worm
hopping like a rabbit
waddling like a duck
rowing a boat
blasting off into orbit
telephoning a friend
swaying like an elephant
driving a car

LANGUAGE dramatics

Most children—even those children with all kinds of developmental disabilities—love dramatics. Not the dramatics with a director who must whip the play into shape for the big performance. No, our dramatics must be spontaneous. Whatever the "actor" wishes to say, whatever the actor wishes to do—it's just fine with us. It is then that the child—every child—begins to feel secure and free. Especially after pantomimes, the children may now feel free and relaxed enough to want to add words to actions:

DIALOGUE

1. Mother is sending you to the store to buy some groceries.
2. You are visiting a sick friend at the hospital.
3. Your little brother spilled a box of marbles all over the floor.
4. You go to welcome the new neighbors who moved in nextdoor.
5. You are collecting the newspaper money from your customers.
6. Some visitors to the city want to know how to get "downtown."
7. You are helping a customer select a new dress.
8. Your dog is missing and you are asking the neighbors if they have seen her.
9. You go to answer the telephone and the caller has the wrong number.
10. You have bought bread and found it was stale. Return it to the store manager.

PLAYS

Impromptu words and actions can be derived from familiar stories:

1. The Milkmaid and Her Pail
2. The Boy Who Cried Wolf
3. The Leak in the Dike
4. Aladdin and His Lamp
5. The Pied Piper of Hamlin
6. The Traveling Musicians
7. William Tell
8. The Emperor's New Clothes

Important historical events and lives of famous people can be made into plays. For example, the Landing of the Pilgrims, the Life of George Washington Carver and Martin Luther King, Jr., and innumerable other fascinating people and events.

LANGUAGE talking time

Sometimes it seems that children get spoken to too much and the precious skills of communicating with others do not get a chance to develop. This is why it's a good idea to have a TALKING TIME period daily (if possible) when children are given a chance to talk.

What can they talk about? Anything—there are no restrictions: a television program, what they did at Grandma's house, what they ate for dinner, their dog or cat, the weather—anything they wish.

Talking time not only helps to develop ease in speaking, it also gives an excellent opportunity to practice the social amenities, the "thank-yous," "you're welcomes," and so on. It may be that the need to teach these amenities is overstressed, but I have found that emphasizing them helps children remember to use them when appropriate.

Talking time also gives children experience in asking questions. Feeling free to ask questions during this period spills over to other experiences. This ability to ask questions is very important for all children; for someday they will be on their own; there will be many things to find out about and learning to ask questions will become a necessity.

Talking time serves another important function for children. Since each child is criticized (favorably or unfavorably) after his or her talk, the child gets experience in learning how to accept criticism gracefully. Since children are convinced that we criticize them because we like them and want them to improve, they come to welcome and accept criticism gracefully. I have seen this happen over and over again.

The following is a sample of a TALKING TIME period. Russell is the "teacher." Each day, a different child has the opportunity to be the "teacher." This procedure may be considered stilted and rigid, but after a short while the children become accustomed to it and follow it quite easily.

RUSSELL: "Will you *please* give us your report?"

DICK: *"Thank you, Russell.* I saw an accident on my way home from school."

RUSSELL: "Would anyone like to ask Dick a question?"

MARY: "What was the accident about?"

DICK: "A car bumped into a bus."

SHARON: "Was anybody hurt?"

DICK: "I don't know because our bus couldn't wait. Mr. Allan thought it might have to be towed in because the gas was leaking out."

(After there are no more questions)

RUSSELL: "Are there any positive comments you would like to make of Dick's report?"

JIM: "I think Dick had a very interesting report."

DICK: *"Thank you, Jim."*

JIM: *"You're welcome, Dick."*

SALLY: "Dick didn't wiggle a lot the way he did yesterday."

DICK: *"Thank you, Sally."*

(After there are no more positive comments)

RUSSELL: "Are there any criticisms? How can we help Dick?"

JOHN: "I think Dick should talk a little louder. I could hardly hear him."

DICK: *"Thank you, John. I will try to talk louder next time."*

JOHN: *"You're welcome, Dick."*

FRED: "When Dick was talking, he looked down at the floor all the time. He should look at us."

DICK: *"Thank you, Fred. I will try to look up next time."*

FRED: *"You're welcome, Dick."*

(After there are no more criticisms)

RUSSELL: *"Thank you* for giving your report, Dick."

DICK: *"You're welcome, Russell."*

RUSSELL: "Who would like to give the next report?"

LANGUAGE art education

Thanks to art reproductions, which can be borrowed from the local art gallery (also from the local library), children can receive loads of added inspiration for talking and writing.

If reproductions are changed each month, there is added aesthetic pleasure as well as the importance of having something worthwhile to talk about and write about.

LANGUAGE newspapers

Children not only enjoy putting out a newspaper—but the practice they get in language development is priceless.

An edition is taken very seriously by the children, who have almost complete responsibility for publication. They fill the jobs of Editor, Business Manager, Advertising Agent, Artist, Designer and Layout personnel, and (of course) Reporter. Every child has a job on the newspaper. Variations of the newspaper can be worked out depending on the ages and abilities of the students.

The rules of punctuation and grammar are enjoyably reinforced in the preparation of the newspaper. The short, crisp, uncomplicated sentence is given a chance to come to life. The children grow to understand the importance of neatness and legibility (for who would want to buy a newspaper that couldn't be read!). The children begin to see a practical need for using the dictionary to look up the proper spelling and meanings of words. The questions of written language become vital since there is a need for them to be taken seriously.

Of even more worth than all these benefits of a newspaper is the behind-the-scenes work by the individual children. It often means disagreements, criticism, doing work all over again, and discouragement, all of which must be done in a cooperative spirit. All of this adds up to a wonderful experience for developing children. You know this unequivocally when you look at the child's face as the child sees the first copy of the paper. It's a glowing look of pride that says, "This is mine! I worked on it!"

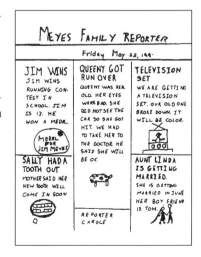

Try a FAMILY REPORTER. With news that is relevant, there is marvelous motivation in language practice.

LANGUAGE field trips

Although there is a steady increase in good reading material for children, making our very own books is something very special indeed! We shall use the world for our subject matter, and we shall go on many, many trips to see this world.

On a trip, our learning becomes alive, three-dimensional, truly meaningful. On a trip all our senses become alive, come into full play—we hear, we smell, we taste, we touch, we see—we grow.

A Field Trip book preserves the academic work that is related to the trip. Each child is given a copy of the book, which then becomes a part of his or her personal library.

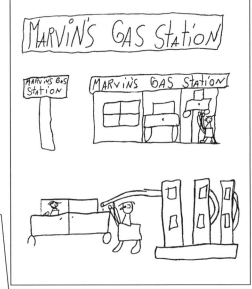

COVER for book on visit to Marvin's Gas Station

THANK YOU letter to Mr. Marvin

194 Elmview Street
Amherst, New York
October 11, 1998

Dear Mr. Marvin,
Thank you for letting our class visit your gas station on October 5, 1991. We saw a lot of the things that you do. We saw how nice you are to the people when they come for gas. Thank you for the cokes you gave all of us.

This was done by your friend,
Aron

WILL BROWN
40 GLEN DRIVE
AMHERST, NEW YORK 14211

Marvins Gas Station
1496 OAK ROAD
Amherst, New York
14226

32¢ STAMP

ENVELOPE in which to mail letter to Mr. Marvin

FIELD TRIPS

Outline

Mr. Marvins Gas Station

I The Gas Station Trip
  A. When: October 5, 1991
  B. Where: 1496 Oak Street
      Town of Herst
      New York
II Mr. Marvin's Work
  A. Puts air in tires
  B. Checks oil and water
  C. Cleans windows
  D. Tells people how to go places
  E. Fixes tires

OUTLINE for composition about visit to Mr. Marvin's gas station

COMPOSITION
developed from outline about the visit

Composition

Mr. Marvin's Gas Station

Our class went To Mr. Marvin's Gas Station, We went on October 5, 1991. The Gas Station is On 1496 Oak Street, Town of Herst.

Mr. Marvin does a lot of Work. He puts air in The Tires. He checks The Oil and water. He cleans The Windows. He Tells people how to go places. He fixes Tires.

READING WORDS related to visit to gas station

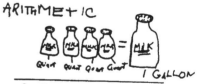

ARITHMETIC WORDS related to visit to gas station

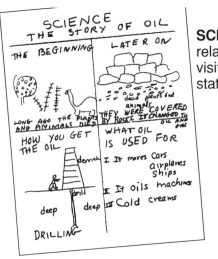

SCIENCE
related to
visit to gas
station

HEALTH
and
SAFETY
tips related
to visit to
gas station

Children will enjoy these trips too:

Zoo
in a big city park
a ten-animal zoo in a small town
a wildlife refuge
a children's zoo with animals
to feed and pet

Pet Store
to see monkeys, hear talking birds, see puppies and kittens

Aquarium
to see fish, turtles, goldfish, sea horses, etc.

SPCA
for homeless, lost, injured, or unwanted animals

Farms
to see (and, hopefully, pet) sheep, cows, horses, pigs, geese, ducks, and other animals. Also to see wheat and corn growing, pear and apple orchards, grape arbors, and so forth. Other farms to try:
a game farm
a wildlife refuge
a dairy farm

Bridges
a bridge across a stream in the park, a rushing river, or between two cities

Locks
to watch the water traffic of large or small boats and ships

Airport
to go on the observation deck to see the loading of passengers and baggage, visit the ticket sales windows, check-in counters, luggage handling, the passenger lounge, restrooms and snack bars. Also the gift shop

Construction Sites
to see buildings going up, roads being laid, ditches being dug or a house being built or demolished, sidewalks or driveways laid, a new lake dredged, water mains installed, telephone wires repaired, electric cables laid

58

Public Buildings   to see the inside and outside, to try out escalators, self-operating elevators, big lobbies, shops in the lobbies

Religious Buildings
   churches
   temples
   mosques
   mission chapels
   store-front churches

Historic Places   a historic home, fort, a pioneer cabin, a first schoolhouse, a colonial village

Still More Trips and Visits
   boat docks
   marinas
   fishing piers
   a lighthouse
   a ferry   *(Try to get a ferry ride.)*
   an old trolley
   old carriages
   a fishing pond *(Can the children go fishing in one and try to catch a real fish?)*
   drive-in movies
   puppet shows
   boat shows
   sailboat races
   swimming pools, wading ponds, beaches
   Native American ceremonials—dances, etc.
   International dance festivals
   Places where people make jewelry, weave baskets, blow glass, dip candles, carve stones
   a spring, a waterfall, rapids, mountains, lakes, beaches, caves, plains, cliffs
   city parks, roadside parks, county parks
   state parks, state forests
   national parks, national monuments, national forests
   historic villages and towns, restored villages
   museums
   special local events—rodeos, folk festivals, street carnivals, apple blossom festivals
   rides on old railroad trains, old trolley cars, rafts, sight-seeing buses, miniature rides in parks or subways
   amusement parks—huge Disneyland or small neighborhood ones

LANGUAGE additional experiences

Ask children, Did you ever hear anyone say, "Be as quiet as a mouse"?
There are lots of other comparisons. They are called SIMILES. Have you
ever heard of these?

Ellen works *like a beaver.*
Mark is *as gentle as a lamb.*
Paula is *as graceful as a swan.*
David is *as hungry as a bear.*
Steven is *as busy as a bee.*
Eric walks *as slow as a turtle.*
Malaika is *as quiet as a mouse.*
Aliya is *as wise as an owl.*

Here are some more SIMILES:

as thin as a rail
as hard as a rock
as fast as lightning
as proud as a peacock
as white as snow
as fit as a fiddle
as easy as pie
as wise as an owl
as fat as a pig
as happy as a lark
as slow as molasses
as quick as a wink

Can you think of any other SIMILES?

Did you ever play the OPPOSITE GAME? Someone says one word and you
think of a word that is altogether different from it (its ANTONYM). Here
are some:

straight (crooked)	boy (girl)
first (last)	high (low)
wide (narrow)	front (back)
hard (soft)	right (left)
happy (sad)	in (out)
sweet (sour)	fat (thin)
night (day)	stand (sit)

Any others?

Can you think of a word that means the same thing as these words, but looks and sounds different?

loud (noisy)	cover (lid)
sick (ill)	baby (infant)
angry (mad)	happy (glad)
thin (skinny)	cry (weep)
insect (bug)	order (command)
farewell (goodbye)	scared (frightened)

Do you know any "GO-TOGETHER" words like:

pen and pencil	Jack and Jill
shoes and socks	pots and pans
salt and pepper	bread and butter
night and day	planes and trains
stop and go	ball and bat
cats and dogs	soap and water
high and low	king and queen

Any more?

Do you have a "family time" at your home (a special time, perhaps after dinner when everybody is home)? It's a good time to take part in conversations like:

What I did today _____

What I think about _____

Some special news event _____

The book you read _____

The movie you saw _____

The baby bird on the sidewalk _____

The birthday party you went to_____

What you did in school today _____

Can you finish these sentences?

I feel happy when _____

I feel sad when_____

I'm scared when _____

I get excited when_____

I like to be by myself when _____

61

Be a poet and make up a short poem with words that rhyme like:

A tiny snail   There was a fish.
crawled out of my pail.   It lived in a dish.

I like to play   The old tree
in the hay.   is the home of the bee.

There are so many, many things to talk about. Why not talk about just YOU?
There is no one in the whole wide world who is just like YOU. Start with:

My name is _____.
I live at _____.
My mother's name is _____.
My father's name is _____.
The names of my sister(s) and brother(s) are

_____.
My friends are _____.
I am happiest when _____.
I just love _____.
I get angry when _____.
I feel afraid when _____.
I like stories when _____.
I want to be _____.
When I was little _____.
I feel proud when _____.
I look forward to _____.
I don't understand why _____.
I like to _____.
If I could do anything I would _____.
If I had three wishes I would _____.
When I grow up I want to _____.

Are there other things you could talk about?

Could you make up a story that took place

at the picnic?
in the attic?
at the play yard?
at the zoo?
in a rainstorm?
on the moon?

62

CITIZEN-SHIP

4. CITIZENSHIP

It is important to instill those character traits and attitudes that make
social living possible
     and
teach the practical facts concerning the community that are important
for successful social living.

If all children were the same, instilling wholesome social living qualities
would be relatively simple for parents and teachers. But every child has
a different mental, social, and emotional background—and so, we
adults have much work to do.

Sometimes a child does not know how to control his or her feelings.
This child might settle an argument with a fistfight. Another child does
not know to cooperate and work constructively in a group. If things do
not go the child's way, this same child will do things that will break up
the group.

When things do not go the child's way, the child becomes intolerant,
raises his or her voice, and resorts to name-calling. Some children will
mark up the walls of the bathroom when no one is looking.

What can we adults do to help instill better social characteristics for
these children? Ideally, this should begin in the home and continue
into the primary grades, and all through the child's formative years.
Unfortunately, we don't always find such good situations. And so, we
have the responsibility to prepare children for social living by working
with the child *where he or she is presently*, using our own resources and
creativity, and creating hundreds of situations from which wholesome
qualities can develop and thrive. Platitudes like "Honesty is the best
policy" won't do it!

A game of checkers could be a "fun" way to encourage good sportsman-
ship.

CITIZENSHIP social characteristics

The importance of TEAMWORK—WORKING TOGETHER FOR THE COMMON GOOD—is fundamental in bringing out the potential for GOOD that is in people. It is a feeling that is particularly valuable in working with children having problems—for they begin to LOOK AT THEMSELVES AND WHAT THEY DO, IN RELATION TO HOW IT AFFECTS OTHER PEOPLE.

"You help me in arithmetic and I'll help you in reading."

"You check me and I'll check you."

Little things can help take children away from their self-centered "me" world and help them feel that they are part of a bigger world of which they are "one of many." Even a "little thing" like a collection of dolls from other countries or a puzzle of the world could be helpful.

CITIZENSHIP meetings

One method of developing a feeling of working TOGETHER is to have MEETINGS. This is a special time set aside each day to examine our own behavior and that of those in the group. If there is a problem, it is brought up at this time. Nothing is too small or insignificant to discuss. The group plugs away at the problem until a satisfactory solution is reached. If it should happen that they reach an impasse, the Leader steps in. No problem is "tabled" or left untouched.

PROBLEMS WHICH CAN BE DISCUSSED AT A MEETING

"Howard ran all the way to gym."

When a child reports on another's misbehavior, this is not considered tattling. Rather, it is bringing this anti-social behavior to the person's attention so that it might be corrected.

We have discussed the kinds of behavior which are socially *useful* and the kinds that are socially *harmful.* We have discussed Rules, and why we have rules in the school, in the home, and in the community. If Howard runs in the slippery hallway, he can fall and hurt himself and he can hurt the people he bumps into, too.

"When we were waiting for the bus, Clifford ran all over the grass."

We have talked about property rights—for *our own* property and that of *others.*

While walking on the grass seems like a small offense, the person is nevertheless being destructive to public property. The person needs to be corrected and told to use the sidewalks instead. He may need to be corrected many times before there is a change in his behavior. Eventually we expect him to understand.

"Anne laughed at my reading."

Ridicule of any kind is not permitted.

"Mrs. Rogovin, you were late for lunch."

Criticism of an adult is encouraged. It is a comforting feeling for the children to know that adults' behavior is not beyond reproach, that they have imperfections and can learn to "improve" too.

"Fred didn't say 'thank you' when I gave out the paste."

Such a small offense may not seem worthy of making an issue, but it helps stress the use of "please," "thank you," and "excuse me." GOOD MANNERS are something children need all their lives.

"I want to criticize myself. Yesterday I didn't feel like doing my homework, so I copied it from Sharon."

Commend children for criticizing themselves. It is not easy for people to look at themselves and admit they were wrong.

"Matthew, your shoes are nice and clean today. They were all full of mud yesterday."

Encourage compliments too!

"I'm the one who took Bob's shoes in gym yesterday. I'm sorry."

Ordinarily, it is difficult for children (and adults) to admit to stealing. But telling the truth is to be encouraged.

It should be noted too, that the person who did something wrong is obliged to say "thank you" to the one who brought the problem before the group. We want the errant person to think, "Your bringing my shortcoming to my attention will help me correct it, and I shall become a better person. This is good. I thank you for this."

CITIZENSHIP collecting stamps

Stamp collecting is an enjoyable leisure time activity and a fine way to broaden children's concept of the world. In addition to collecting the stamps from the mail their own family receives, they are encouraged to collect from their friends and neighbors.

Stamps are likely to show up from all places of the world, places children may not have known exist.

CITIZENSHIP telephone

"Not know how to dial a telephone number? Such a simple thing!" Yes, it is simple for most children. But for some with less ability, it is not simple! And this is only one part of telephone usage.

Children need to know: how to answer a phone properly
how to take telephone messages properly
how to ask for information
how to make calls from a telephone booth
and how to use the phone for personal needs.

Adults and teachers can teach this to students, but sometimes a representative from a telephone company can do an even better job. Children in the classroom love to use telephone training equipment and compare how "awful" they sound at first to the "great" improvement they make later.

At home, children can use a toy handset to practice "making calls":

MY TELEPHONE LiST	
MY NAME IS JERRY	
MY NUMBER IS	632-4872
EMERGENCY	
FIRE	632-1110
DOCTOR	632-4763
POLICE	632-3311
MOTHERS JOB	632-9986
FATHER'S JOB	632-9602
SHOPPING	
BiLL'S GROCERY	632-4610
FEDERAL MEAT	632-4961
FRIENDS	
TOM	632-2741
BILL	632-0429

Shirley's mother is not well. Call Father at work.

Order some food from the corner grocery store.

A fire started at the kitchen stove. Call the fire department.

Call up Sam to go fishing with you on Sunday.

You see someone looking inside your bedroom window. Call the police station.

Find out the telephone number of your doctor. Can you get "information"?

When does the bus leave for New York City?

All the children should have a telephone list and learn to use it with ease.

CITIZENSHIP police department

The image of today's police is forever needing a boost. They are not often thought of as persons who endanger their lives to protect our homes, who keep our streets safe, and whom we can call in emergencies.

Getting to know a police officer can help. If the officer knows young people well and how to communicate with them, he or she can talk their language to explain

>   laws
>   why we have laws
>   the need for everybody's cooperation
>   the dangers of drinking, drugs, etc.

The officer's visit to us is followed by our visit to police headquarters, where the children have a chance to see everything: the cell block, the gun room, the line-up room, and so forth.

Mementos from our visit to the police headquarters give us many things to talk about.

CITIZENSHIP fire safety

Sometimes children do not have enough fire-safety instructions. Too often instructions are given sporadically, depending on some special campaign or a dramatic fire involving the loss of life. And if children become confused and stunned when they hear the fire-drill bell, what might they do in a real emergency?

As a result, our class has monthly instruction in fire safety. One lesson includes a visit to a nearby fire station. Another lesson includes a classroom visit by a fire fighter. Other lessons include:

1)   Walks *within* the schools to locate the EXIT signs and FIRE-ALARM BOXES

2)   Walks *outside* the school to locate the FIRE-ALARM BOX and FIRE HYDRANT

3)   The enactment of dramatizations to show ways of preventing fire and what to do in case of fire.

NEW WORDS
① fire
② fire — man
③ fire — station
④ fire — proof
⑤ fire — engine
⑥ safety
⑦ hose
⑧ burn

"No . . . ALMOST OUT will not do when you put out a fire. A fire is out only when you can press your hand against the spot where the fire was!" says a visiting firefighter.

Fire-fighter's tools

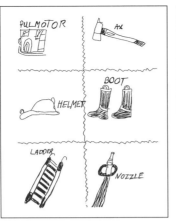

CITIZENSHIP maps

Children do not always have a sense of location. Beginning by making a simple map of the street where they live, they can advance to a two-block stretch. Later, to a neighborhood, town, or city. (When a larger space is needed, try working on an old, unused window shade.)
Because we do not wish to clutter children's minds with abstract details, only useful information is included:

the firebox
the mailbox
the police or emergency box
the library
the school

the church
the doctor's office
stores for shopping
the police station
the hospital or clinic

THE SOCIETY FOR PREVENTION OF CRUELTY TO ANIMALS

"No, we just don't have any more room for pets," I protested as we came to the cage of darling kittens during our visit to the new SOCIETY FOR PREVENTION OF CRUELTY TO ANIMALS building. But the pleas of the children were more than I could handle and, before long, Blacky and Brownie were placed in a box to come home with us. Somehow we found room for them, and I'm glad we did for the pleasures and learning experiences they gave us were more than I had counted on!

There are many, many more Blackys and Brownies (dogs, birds, white mice) at the SPCA. I heartily suggest that teachers and parents hurry to get at least one of them!

MULTICULTURAL CENTERS

I remember having seen a very fine film called *The Brave One*. In it the young son of a Native American woman is killed and she is crying. A white man looks on, surprised at this. It never occurred to him before, that Native Americans, too, have feelings and they, too, love their children!

Many more such films and much more education are still needed to eliminate the deep-rooted prejudices that people have. Unless they are taught otherwise, children inevitably absorb attitudes of prejudice.

Books, films, cultural fairs, and centers for diversity help us educate children to accept and enjoy racial differences. Their members— Asians, African Americans, and Native Americans—come to visit us and as a result we begin to hear such comments as, "They're awful nice" and "they're just like us." They discover by themselves that the differences are superficial—different clothes, hair style, the language, and some different ways of doing things.

72

MUSEUM OF SCIENCE

The world is too much with us; late and soon,
Getting and spending, we lay waste our powers:
Little we see in Nature that is ours.

These lines were written well over a century ago by the poet Wordsworth. What would he say now with our polluted waters and air, the superhighways that invade much of our forests, and little children brought up with artificial flowers in their homes instead of the fragrance of real ones?

Children need such institutions as museums of science more than ever! Here, the wonders of nature are exposed so that they can be examined closely and marveled at. Butterflies, birds, a buffalo, an anteater, a room showing us how man the human being evolved, fossils of plants and animals millions of years old, wildflowers we may look at but never pick. All this and much more!

Unlike most conventional classes, classes at museums are primarily for "doing":

> hiking in the woods
> collecting stones or fossils
> making totem poles
> learning Native American dances, etc.

A diorama of Africa *(borrowed from our museum)* gave my class background material for the study and appreciation of citizens of African heritage. Our concern was not how much subject matter could be taught about Africa but, What would the child *learn* from this activity?

> Does the child see relationships between the child's way of life and someone else's?
> Do the children develop a respect for others even though they do things differently?
> Finally, will they better understand African American citizens in the community?

73

Following are pages from booklets made by students after field trips to museums and other community institutions.

Mrs. Clemans

Mrs. Clemans showed us many interesting things. She was kind. She told us interesting stories. I think that she likes kids a lot.

That is a Buffalo

LIVE ANIMAL ROOM

I liked the live animal room best of all because my hobby is animals. All the other boys liked this room too.

Duck Alligator Mouse Fish Porcupine Snake

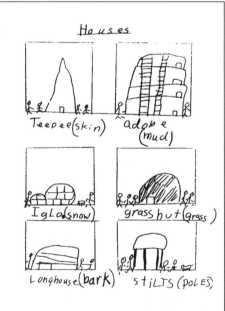

Houses

Teepee (skin)   adobe (mud)

Igloo (snow)   grass hut (grass)

Longhouse (bark)   stilts (poles)

The Hall of Man.

We saw The Hall of Man. We saw how we look inside. We are like a big factory. All The parts have to work OK or you get sick.

74

The Gun Room

They had many different kind of guns.
They had old fashioned army guns. They had bayonets on some of the guns.
We saw a boot lake gun.
It was called a boot — gun because it was carried in the boots.

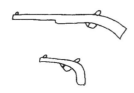

The Car Room

The old cars were funny to see. It was funny to see how they changed. I liked the old black one, Mrs. Moore said it still ran. I liked the coaches too. It would be great to go for a long trip on one. I liked the bicycles too. The red car ran on batteries.

The Flag Case

We saw the flags of the wars. The flags of the Civil War were worn out. We saw the flags of World War I. They were used when my parents were young. We saw the flags of World War II. My mother's brother was killed in World War II. I hope we don't have anymore wars again.

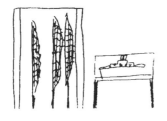

SAND - PAINTING

The Indians sand - paint.
IF They want it to Rain They make a sand-painting. If someone is sick They make a sand painting. It is like praying.

MR. MASTERSON

Mr Masterson is our Scout Leader. He is a swell man. He shows us how to make knots, He tells us how to be good scouts. We have a lot of fun with him.

A Scout is kind

This means that a Scout is good to people. This means he is good to dogs he likes to be nice to everybody.

A SCOUT IS BRAVE

This means that a Scout wants to help Other People. He wants to help even if there is danger.

A Scout is Trustworthy

This means that a Scout can be trusted. He won't take things that don't belong to him.

The title of this booklet is "IF." Other pages include, "If everyone were white instead of black, red, or mixed." "If everyone were Catholic instead of Jewish, Protestant, or Islamic," etc. The booklet ends with, ". . . WHAT A DULL WORLD IT WOULD BE!"

The top of this booklet shows THE WRONG WAY TO BE, and the bottom shows THE RIGHT WAY TO BE.

The title of this booklet is "TREAT OTHER PEOPLE THE WAY YOU WOULD LIKE OTHER PEOPLE TO TREAT YOU."

These are pages from a BROTHERHOOD BOOKLET called "IT'S WHAT'S INSIDE OF YOU THAT COUNTS."

Other pages are "Some people are Polish, Italian, Spanish—IT'S WHAT'S INSIDE OF YOU THAT COUNTS." "Some people live in big houses and have lots of things. Some people live in little houses and don't have lots of things—IT'S WHAT'S INSIDE OF YOU THAT COUNTS."

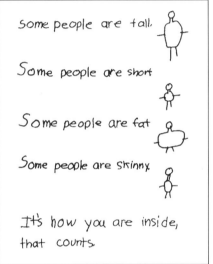

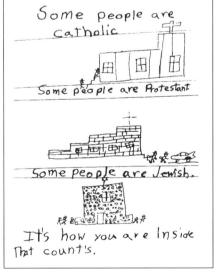

CITIZENSHIP job preparation

Practicing job interviews helps to make the first real interview less traumatic.

WRONG WAY

Boss: How do you do, Mr. Merrill.
Russell: Hi!
Boss: How are you?
Russell: Aw—I got a lot of troubles.
Boss: What is your age?
Russell: Old enough.
Boss: What grade are you in?
Russell: I quit school.
Boss: What kind of job are you interested in?
Russell: Anything I kin get hold of. As long as it's easy.
Boss: How much do you expect to get?
Russell: The more the better.
Boss: When would you want to start?
Russell: Maybe in a couple weeks . . . when I quit my other job . . . No hurry.
Boss: Thank you for coming in, Mr. Merrill. I'll call you when I need you.
Russell: So long.

RIGHT WAY

Boss: How do you do, Mr. Merrill.
Russell: How do you do, Mr. Schwartz.
Boss: How are you?
Russell: Fine, Mr. Schwartz and how are you?
Boss: What is your age?
Russell: I am 16 years old. My birthday is August 4.
Boss: What grade are you in?
Russell: I am a sophomore at high school.
Boss: What kind of job are you interested in?
Russell: I would like to deliver groceries.
Boss: How much do you expect to get an hour?
Russell: I would like to get experience. I will take whatever you can afford to give.
Boss: When would you like to start work?
Russell: I would start any time you like.
Boss: Thank you for coming in, Mr. Merrill. You seem like you would be a good worker. You can start tomorrow at 3 P.M.
Russell: Thank you, Mr. Schwartz. I'll be there at 3. Thank you. Goodbye.

AUTOMATION and increased SPECIALIZATION have made sizable dents in the labor market. Yet, for a long time to come, there may still be demand for:

Laundry workers	Window cleaners
Charwomen	Cafeteria workers
Supermarket stock clerks	Porters
Car washers	Fountain clerks
Gardeners' helpers	Farmhands
Moving van loaders	Janitors' helpers
Nurses' aides	Canning factory workers

The object in JOB TRAINING is to develop those characteristics that are necessary for job holding and background that prepares the student to make job choices with some understanding. We study the requirements of a job.

> What is expected of the worker?
> How much reading and writing is expected?
> Will the job require a health checkup?
> Will the job have many responsibilities or just one?
> Will the worker need to wear a uniform?
> What are the hours of work?

We study the student's individual characteristics, which may be more suited for one type of job than another.

> Does the child like to work alone or with other people?
> Does the child make a good appearance or is the child inclined to look sloppy?
> Does the child dawdle or does the child go about work industriously?
> Can the child handle a heavy physical job or one that is "light"?

We study the GOOD ASPECTS of a job and the BAD ASPECTS of a job.

> Is the work indoors or outdoors?
> Is the work regular or part-time?
> Is it a "dirty" job or a "clean" job?
> Is the job on a "shift" that the applicant prefers?
> Is the salary satisfactory?

When the topic is job training, every phase is directed toward the development of those characteristics (cooperation, trustworthiness, obedience, etc.) which will make the child or student successful on the job.

Adults are treated respectfully.
Small responsibilities are taken seriously.

CITIZENSHIP Social Security

When the child "passes" the job training requirements *in* the class-room, the child is ready to go *outside* the classroom (to other parts of the building) for bigger challenges. There will be less familiar grounds, a new "boss," and different responsibilities.

As Librarian's Assistant, for example, the child

1. waters the plants.
2. straightens chairs.
3. returns books and magazines to their proper places.
4. helps the librarian "check out" books.

History books tell us that the government used to give away (!) 160 acres of free land to any person who wished to be a farmer. It is possible that this was an early kind of Social Security. What a contrast compared with our life today! Present-day Social Security protects against risks that are common to all, risks against which individuals would be unable to provide adequate safeguards.

The basic system for old age, survivors, disability, and health insurance (Medicare) now covers practically all persons who work for a living! As soon as a person goes to work on the first paying job, he or she becomes a part of this system.

What do children need to know?

1) how and when a person gets a Social Security card
2) how to care for the card
3) what to do if the card gets lost.

CITIZENSHIP unions

STRIKE
PICKET LINE
UNION SHOP
INJUNCTION
FRINGE BENEFITS
SENIORITY

These are words commonly used in general conversation, newspapers, radio, and television. Children need to know about unions. If given a good background in the principles of "unionism" (its early history stemming from inhumane child-labor practices, long working hours, sweatshop working conditions, etc.), children are more likely to take "unionism" seriously.

An explanation of unions can help children understand that if workers want one thing and bosses want another thing, the best thing to do is to sit down and try to work out the problem together.

Talking with a union member or a union organizer is a wonderful way to learn about unions.

CITIZENSHIP workers' compensation

Some children are "accident-prone." It may be hard for some people to understand, but there are some children who may stand on a ladder or a box without considering whether or not it will hold them. Some may hurry at work heedlessly and cause an accident. Some children, if they grow confused, may stop what they are doing and so cause an accident. Some children get numb and frightened when they see a sign of danger. There are so many ways everyone can have accidents!

And so, it becomes extremely important to find out as much as possible about WORKERS' COMPENSATION:

1. how to report an injury
2. where to get the proper forms
3. how to fill out the form

CITIZENSHIP banking

Many children are good at squandering their earnings. There are others who would even hide their earnings under a pillow for safekeeping! This is why we study all we can about banking.

Although many schools have a banking program, the "transactions" are quite limited. It is easy to set up a banking program at home.

> The children make real deposits of money (however small) and at regular times (once a week).
>
> They fill out real deposit and withdrawal slips.
>
> They keep records in a real passbook.
>
> They learn to write real checks, endorse them, and keep records of them.

Also try a safe deposit vault (a small box with a key) for "valuables," another box earmarked "Christmas Club money," and a third for "vacations."

The children are allowed to borrow money from the bank (for a small interest rate of one or two cents), but *only* if there is a legitimate need for it.

CITIZENSHIP life insurance

It is difficult for most children to "see ahead." It is hard, for example, to conceive of the fact that they may someday be seriously ill with tremendous doctor and hospital bills to pay, that there may be a fire in the home, that a big windstorm can blow off the roof of the back porch, or that a passerby may slip on the ice in front of their home and get hurt. Whether children can "see" these eventualities or not, they must be prepared to meet them when they do come.

Children can learn to understand the basic principle of insurance, that the pooling of contributions of many people makes possible the ability to meet the expenses incurred by individual members of the group. It can be shown that the principle of "prepayment" of medical expenses is possible because (though no one knows whether John Jones will get appendicitis this year or not) insurance companies *can estimate how many such cases* will occur in any group of one hundred John Joneses.

How much fun the children can have "taking out" fire, automobile, life, homeowner, and health insurance policies. (Of course, we make sure that all payments are made on time!)

CITIZENSHIP home buying

One might wonder why children need to know about real estate. Yet, it is possible that these same children may be homeowners someday.

At one time, home ownership was generally limited to the wealthy. Now we see millions of homes owned by those in low-income and middle-income families. Some may work in factories where wages are relatively good. Some persons hold two jobs. A working husband and a working wife bring in two incomes. If a house is going to be purchased, what are the questions that need to be considered?

A person who works in real estate can help children understand basic questions related to buying a house:

Can I afford the house (consideration of earnings, down payment, upkeep, etc.)?
What is the condition of the house (consideration of furnace, hot-water tank, roof, plaster, etc.)?
Is the location satisfactory (consideration of nearness to schools, shopping, parks, and playgrounds)?

If buying a house is out of the question, what needs to be known about renting?

What are the advantages? the disadvantages?
What is included in the rent (gas, electricity, a garage, etc.)?
Is there a lease?

READING

ONEWAY

5. READING

There's a lot of concern about the matter of reading—why so many children aren't good readers and why so many children don't like to read. There are many studies on these matters—and it is important to try to get at the causes of these problems.

I personally have found that virtually every parent wants his or her child to learn to read and to like reading. Children are sent off to school with the parents' high hopes. But then, after a while we often find many of these same children reading below and even far below their potential. I have seen this happen over and over again.

Perhaps there really are no definitive answers to this problem. I have often wondered about these questions:

1. Is the child mature enough to learn to read? The fact that children have the same chronological age does not mean they have the same maturity. Experienced adults have seen little boys often six months to a year less mature than little girls of the same age. Nevertheless, all the little girls and all the little boys start at the same time!
2. If forced to read before the little child is mature enough, this same child can become more proficient at avoiding reading than reading! Most of us know the techniques—daydreaming, looking out the window, spitballs, doodling, and so forth.
3. Is the child motivated to want to read? Is there a strong desire to read? This matter of "desire" may be more clearly seen when the parent insists that the child learn to play the piano, even though the child doesn't want to learn to play the piano. (We all know too well what happens to the lessons after a while!)
4. Sometimes it's important to stop and ask ourselves:
   * Do our children see that reading is important to our lives?
   * Do they see that when we want to relax, we choose to pick up a book to read?
   * Do they see that when we want to get some information about something, we can find it in a book?
   * Do they see us going to the library, and do we take the child along with us?
   Attitudes are very contagious!

5. Have all the potential physical handicaps been checked out: Vision? Hearing?
6. Have all the potential mental conditions been checked out? Does the child have a "normal" mental ability? Does the child have any developmental disabilities such as mental retardation? autism?
7. Does the child have any background in "phonics" (see following pages)?
8. Does the child have any background at all in "sight words" (see following pages)?

Unless "Yes" can be answered to most of these questions, it is possible that the results in reading may not be very positive.

READING phonics

Have you ever watched a poor reader read or try to read? The child looks at the letter "m" (for example) and doesn't know that the lips have to be pursed to make the "mmmm" sound. The child looks at the vowel "a" and doesn't know that there is a "hard a" and a "soft a"; nor does the child know the rules for following them. The child is stymied when confronted with a word beginning with "wr" or "th" because the rules of how to make these sounds have never been taught the child. The child is often "stuck" with an unfamiliar word because the child was never taught (at the right time) the step-by-step approach to reading. Without this preparation, the child does not have the "power" to figure out how the word is pronounced. The child needs to know how to take a word apart and put it together.

PHONICS (the sounds of the letters of the alphabet) goes out of fashion every once in a while, and the wonderful system of "sounding" is replaced with "progressive" reading techniques. Many commercial book manufacturers often flood the market with "progressive" reading books.

Books like the old "Dick and Jane" books (for example) mostly depended on

how well the child was able to memorize
how well the child was able to "figure" out the word by its context.

The ability to figure out the word independently is not always given to a child except by some understanding adult who may have avoided the term "phonics" and continued to teach the developmental steps nevertheless.

Fortunately, phonics is making something of a comeback nowadays. When a child, taught slowly and systematically, looks at a word, figures out its parts, and is able to put them back together, reading can turn out to be very exciting!

It's always been a mystery to me why there is such resistance to the use of the phonetic approach to reading, especially since the majority of our words can be pronounced phonetically. It's so useful to children because it is a reliable approach and can be depended on. As the child succeeds, the child gains confidence. It's quite true that there are rules to follow, but not many. Here are some basic steps:

1. These are 15 CONSONANTS that always sound as they are written:

    B D F H J K L M N P R S T V W

2. Q Z X and beginning Y make SPECIAL SOUNDS:

    Q says kw as in *quit, queen* (Q is always followed by U).
    Z says Zz as in *zoo, zero.*
    X says ks as in *ax, box.*
    Y says yy as in *yes, yellow.*

3. C and G:

    C followed by A or O or U says K as in *call, come, cut.*
    C followed by I or Y or E says S as in *city, fancy, cell.*
    G followed by A or O or U says G as in *go, gave, gum.*
    G followed by I or Y or E often changes the sound to J as in *giant, gypsy, gem.*

4. CONSONANT COMBINATIONS (two consonants often seen together as the beginning of a word):

gr as in *grin*	fl as in *flat*	st as in *star*
pr as in *pretty*	bl as in *black*	sp as in *spot*
fr as in *from*	gl as in *glad*	spr as in *spring*
tr as in *tree*	br as in *brown*	str as in *strong*

5. FOUR BLENDS (Do not take these letters apart. Sound them together):

    ch as in *chair*
    sh as in *ship*
    wh as in *what*
    th as in *the*

6. VOWELS (90 percent of our words are made up of SHORT vowel sounds):

a as in *apple*
e as in *bed*
i as in *in*
o as in *on*
u as in *fun*
y (sometimes) If there is no other vowel, the Y is sure to be a vowel
sound, and it says i-i-i as in *my, cry, by.*

7. VOWELS (LONG)

When there are two vowels, the first says its own name and the second
vowel is silent as in *ate, hate, pine.*

When there are two vowels together in the middle of a word, the second is silent as in coat, pail, seal, bean.

8. SPECIAL SOUNDS

al as in *all*   aw as in *saw*   ur as in *hurt*
ar as in *car*   er as in *her*   oi as in *oil*
ow as in *cow*   ir as in *fir*   oy as in *boy*

Reading sight words

Reputable reading specialists tell us that between 50 to 75 percent of ordinary reading material boils down to a basic list of such common, everyday words as "the," "and," "a" plus about 200 to 250 others. (This ought to be a happy thought, when you consider the size of the average dictionary!)

Adults can purchase a set of these basic "sight words," and drill whenever possible so that the child knows the word automatically—when the word is seen—and doesn't have to try to figure out the word. It pops out of the child automatically. (There is no need to stop with, "Now let me see—what is that word?")

Why not make or purchase a set of sight word cards. Let the child have the pack and play games with it.

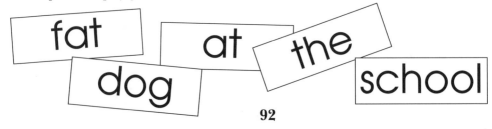

WHO OR WHAT WORDS	HOW IT LOOKS WORDS
mother	little
father	big
girl	pretty
boy	funny
baby	good
house	cold
school	hot
children	old
ball	small
dog	fat

WHERE WORDS	
in	over
on	away
up	to
under	here
down	out

COLOR WORDS	NUMBERS
red	one
blue	two
green	three
yellow	four
white	five
black	six
brown	seven
	eight
	nine
	ten

This is part of a made-up list of "sight words." Notice how common and "every-day-ish" these words are.

Sight words can be put together to form common phrases.

Reading phonograms

Remember the phonograms on which many of us drilled years ago? Imagine what fun it could be for a child to be able to make hundreds of words just by hitching some letters to a "family":

PREFIX	SUFFIX
ab	s
em	ed
en	er
ex	est
in	ing
out	en
un	

AD	AG	AIL	AKE	ALL	AME	AN	AND
had	bag	fail	bake	ball	came	ban	band
dad	nag	jail	cake	call	game	can	hand
bad	rag	mail	lake	fall	lame	fan	land
mad	sag	sail	make	hall	name	man	sand
sad	wag	tail	take	tall	same	pan	stand

ANK	AP	AT	ATCH	E	EAR	EAT	EST
bank	cap	bat	batch	be	dear	beat	best
drank	lap	cat	catch	he	hear	cheat	chest
sank	nap	fat	hatch	me	fear	heat	nest
tank	rap	hat	match	she	near	meat	rest
thank	tap	mat	patch	we	year	seat	test

ICK	ILL	IN	ING	OOL	OLD	OP	UMP
brick	bill	bin	ding	cool	cold	cop	bump
kick	fill	pin	king	fool	fold	drop	dump
lick	hill	sin	ring	pool	gold	hop	jump
pick	mill	thin	sing	school	hold	mop	pump
sick	pill	win	thing	tool	sold	stop	rump

Why not use these same lists to help with spelling too!

READING incidental reading

Pictures can deliberately be placed about, in hope that the child will become curious about the words and want to learn them.

The added stimulation of having "experienced" (seen) words on a field trip can mean the words are more likely to be learned.

COMMON SIGNS

Who knows how many of these common signs will be of importance to one of our children? Learning to read them could be very important someday.

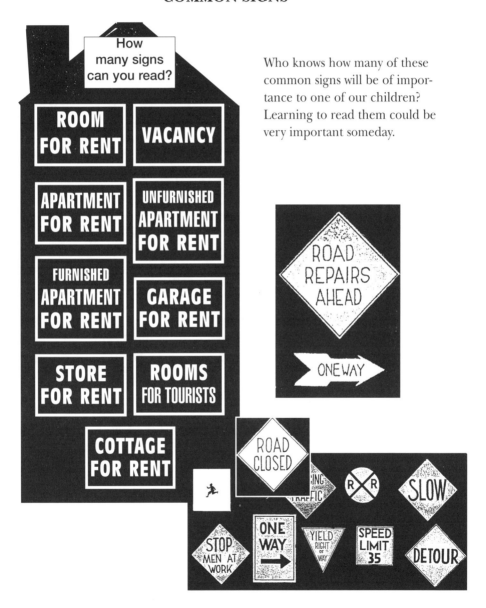

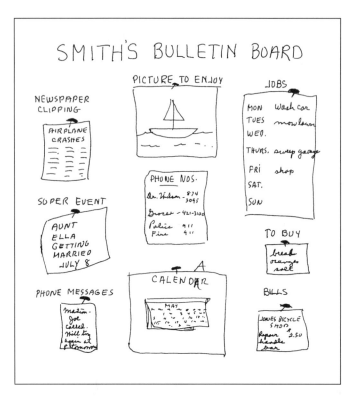

A **FAMILY BULLETIN BOARD** can motivate a student to read.

Try a **FAMILY REPORTER**. With news that is relevant, the child is highly motivated to read.

News can include original poems, jokes, coming events, etc.

READING reading corner

One of the worst things you can tell a child is "Go read a book." When such demands are made on children, after a while many of them inwardly begin to fear the sight of a book. (Did you ever see a child pretend to read, knowing that it would please an adult?)

Why not set up a pleasant spot in a corner of a room, a spot made so attractive that a child will be lured to it. Even if the child goes there only to look at the pictures in the books, this is a good beginning.

Try to get easy-to-read books for the Reading Corner. Offer books below the reading level of the child. (A young child who complains, "Gee, this book is so-o-o easy!" may begin to feel that it is a pleasure to read without a struggle. It's good to experience the feeling of reading easily.)

READING library

Often one person is in charge of "story hour" at the library each week. The way she reads and the exciting selection of books lures the children, who feel they really "don't want to miss" going. (Sometimes she reads a book a chapter at a time, one chapter each week—and that makes the child not want to miss!)

For some children, a library could well be a forbidding place, especially with thousands of books lining the walls. A regular weekly visit can help to overcome this negative feeling, and (before long) the library is seen as a warm, friendly place where everyone is always welcome.

One can go there to relax a bit, just look at magazines, pick out a book to take home—or just chat with the friendly librarian.

When the child has learned how to care for books and the proper library discipline, why not take out a library card and let the child enjoy being a library member.

READING reading games

Learning to read can't be all play, but much of it can be learned through play.

A word domino game can be made from construction paper, tagboard, cork—or, more permanently—from wood blocks.

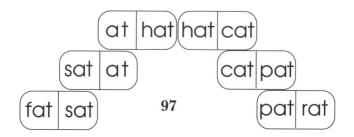

"ZOETROPE"

You can make a "Zoetrope" from a shoe box. "Film" can be made from comic strips, magazine pictures, groups of your favorite friends, movie stars, or baseball players. Whatever you choose, everything looks quite special when you peep at it inside a shoe box.

A sewing card can be a fun way to reinforce a new reading word.

Pictures can be drawn or cut out of magazines.

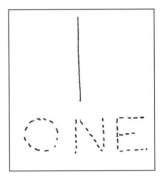

Use colored yarn to sew the word. (Be sure the needle is blunt.)

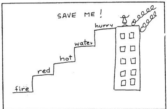

EASY DRAWINGS

Easy-to-make drawings encourage children to look forward to reading. You don't have to be an artist to make these silly little drawings. However crude, they attract children and encourage them to work (though they call it "play").

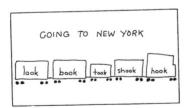

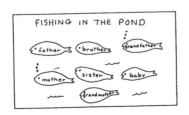

Reading notebooks

Children can make their own notebooks of related words.
Notebooks can be made using categories such as:

animals
parts of the body
clothing
holidays
furniture
movement (walking,
    running, jumping,
    etc.)
people from other lands
stores
well-known people
community helpers

Children can make notebooks of the related sounds letters make. Notebooks
can be made for:

vowel sounds for "A" *(cat, bag, man)*
vowel sounds for "E" *(egg, bed, tent)*
vowel sounds for "O" *(pot, doll, top)*
consonant sounds for "S" *(sit, stop,
    soup, ads)*

TO ENCOURAGE READING, SHOW A CHILD HOW TO MAKE ACCORDION BOOKS

Pages (cards) can be taped end-to-end vertically.

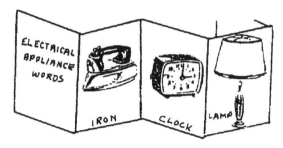

Pages (cards) can be taped end-to-end horizontally.

Cards (pages) can be taped together without any folds.

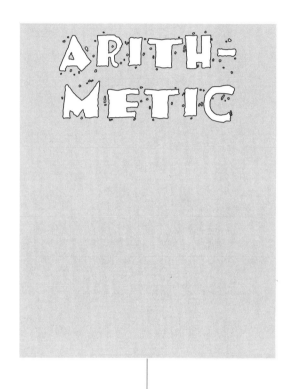

6

6. ARITHMETIC

"Has this material been important and indispensable to me in my own life?" This is always the question I must ask myself before deciding what to teach students in arithmetic.

Actually—when we stop to think about it—there isn't really a great deal of arithmetic that we use in everyday living . . . some addition, subtraction, multiplication, division for everyday business transactions . . . some simple measurements . . . "how to tell time" . . . a few of the easier fractions . . .

Happily, this means we can eliminate much of the traditional arithmetic from our curriculum. After all, what point is there in trying to teach $\frac{3}{8} + \frac{7}{8}$ or $\frac{7}{8} \times 32$ when it is much more important to know how much change to expect when a clerk is given \$1 for a 10¢ pencil.

In teaching arithmetic to children, I find that any method by which correct results can be reached is a good method. Though it may be considered heresy, the students who have a great deal of difficulty with number sense are allowed to use their fingers if they wish. Better to use fingers and get the correct answer than not to and be wrong. Besides, some are able to use their fingers very rapidly!

ARITHMETIC playing store

Many, many children are literal-minded. These children seem to learn best when material is presented to them in situations in which concrete objects are used, in which we always try to approximate a real situation as closely as possible. And so, if they need to know about "buying and selling," they "play store."

When their "store" is conducted like any small neighborhood store, the children have palatable experiences, learning to:

> figure costs
> make change
> use sales slips
> keep accounts
> stay within budget
> use good manners, etc.

They can take turns being the storekeeper, customer, or check-out cashier.

Periodic "sales" give highly motivational lessons in subtraction, percentages, and so forth, for the more advanced students.

To play "store":

Merchandise can be empty cereal boxes, rinsed out cans, etc.
A table can be the check-out counter.
A doll carriage can be the shopping cart.
Play money can be cut from paper (an egg carton can be the cash register), though it may be better to use real money.

You can buy ready-made stores, but children like to use their own ingenuity. For example, this pharmacy was made by emptying a small bookcase and setting it above a table. While stock for the store can be purchased, I have found that children are much more interested in cartons, cans, and containers that have been used and brought from home. They only need to be emptied, washed, and furnished with "price" labels.

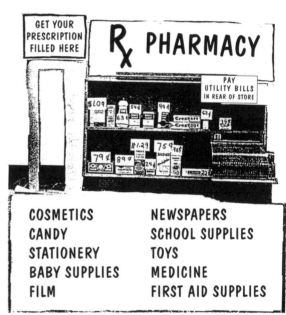

The cardboard core of a waxpaper box or a toilet tissue roll becomes the telephone and we are open for business! Gas, electric, and telephone bills are paid at the pharmacy too.

Children can make any kind of store found in a neighborhood or shopping plaza, a hardware store, department store, shoe store, and many others. Any of these give opportunity to familiarize them with new units of measure and special terminology associated with them. All we have to do is change the name, gather together the appropriate stock, and make out new price tags!

MAKING CHANGE

We also use "real money," which means that nothing has to be unlearned or relearned at a later date. Because knowing how to buy things and "get change" is a *must* for everyday living, using "real money" is given top priority in math work.

CAN YOU MAKE CHANGE?		
PENNY	(coin)	
NICKLE	(coin)	(coin) (coin) (coin) (coin) (coin)
DIME	(coin)	(coin) (coin)
QUARTER	(coin)	(coin) (coin) (coin)

ROMAN NUMERALS

Give a child a supply of wooden toothpicks and see how eagerly the child will want to make roman numerals. The child may learn all the numbers up to 12 (which is enough for reading the roman numerals on a clock). If the child is willing and adept, it will be fun to go all the way to 20 (which is more than enough for general use).

ARITHMETIC measurements

Slower or shy children may sit like cups waiting to be filled. "Learning by doing" helps bring them into activity. For example, children can use sand or sawdust to find out about DRY MEASURE. (However, they usually prefer the use of luscious apples for their experiments!) LIQUID

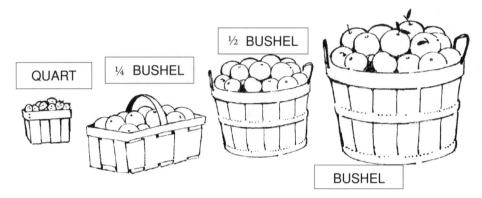

MEASURE can be more easily understood and more appealing if the liquid happens to be some delicious grape or pineapple juice!

Why not find out about can sizes (gallons, pints, etc.) by using actual cans? It will make it easier for some children to remember them.

ARITHMETIC charts

"In one ear and out the other." This sometimes seems to be the way some children's minds work. A child can be sent to the store to get a few items, and (if not written down) one, some, or all of the items are forgotten. Some children seem to have a lot of trouble following simple directions in making something or going somewhere—it seems that the spoken word takes little or no hold on the child's mind.

And so, why not use the motto, "Don't just tell the child—show the child!" One very effective technique involves the use of CHARTS. A chart can take main points, simplify them, dramatize them, and make the information easier to absorb.

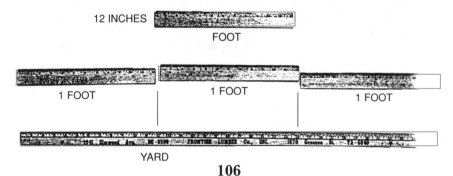

ARITHMETIC shapes

A child can have so much fun with shapes like triangles, rectangles, squares, circles.

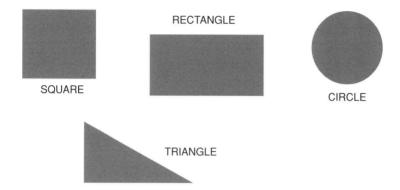

- Shapes can be cut from colored paper and sorted into piles.
- Shapes can be made into designs or figures, like a human figure, a tree, abstract patterns, etc.
- Look for shapes around the house—for example, the circles of a clock, buttons, saucers, etc.
- Look for shapes on a walk—for example, the rectangular shape of a window or the triangular shape of an evergreen tree.

DOZEN

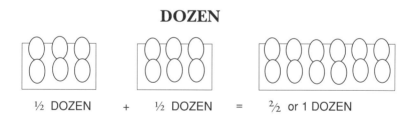

½ DOZEN   +   ½ DOZEN   =   ²⁄₂ or 1 DOZEN

FRACTIONS

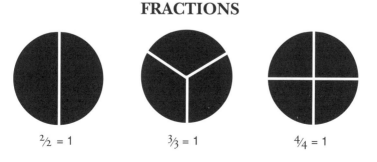

$^2/_2 = 1$ $^3/_3 = 1$ $^4/_4 = 1$

LINES

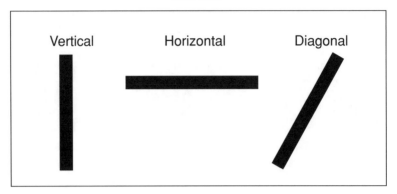

Vertical   Horizontal   Diagonal

Lines generally run in different directions, and it's usually easier for a child to understand this using an illustration, such as the one above.

ARITHMETIC newspapers

Of course, there are dozens and dozens of commercially published math workbooks for children. But how much more exciting it is for children to get their practice using the daily newspaper! Math problems derived from the newspaper are alive and pertinent to their lives. Here children see reasons to want to learn addition, subtraction, multiplication, (discount) percentages, and more.

This day-to-day association with newspaper ads encourages children to notice when the price of eggs, milk, and other commodities changes. (The ads also dramatize the need for "comparative shopping.")

SAVE .40
Crick's
Cottage Cheese
16 oz. Small Curd,
Large Curd
or Low Fat
(Dairy Dept.)
.88

Save .30
Wegs
Orange Juice
12 oz. can
(makes 48 fl. oz.)
.99

SAVE .98
Mannas
Ice Cream
Two H gallon (all reg. var
(Frozen Dept.)
2 for 3.00

See how exciting the potentialities are in these newspaper ads!

25%-50% OFF
BOYS' CLOTHING

Shirts, pants, sweaters, tees, and more from many manufacturers. Sizes 4-20.

Reg. $10-$90 SALE $7.50-$68

SPECIAL PURCHASE

599

Comp. Value: 11.95

YOU SAVE 50%

WOMEN'S DRESS SLINGS Black patent dress slings gives your wardrobe a fall fashion flair.

ARITHMETIC personal data

"When is your birthday?" "What is your phone number?" These are such common questions. Yet, if a child is not taught them, answers may well be "I don't know."

In order to learn pertinent personal information, a child can be given a form called "MY PERSONAL RECORD." It can be made of cardboard and made ready for practice or quick reference.

MY PERSONAL RECORD

NAME	NAN NOGAL
ADDRESS	
STREET	2 NORTH ST.
CITY	BUFFALO
STATE	NEW YORK
ZIP CODE	14212
BIRTHDAY	
MONTH	MAY
DAY	2
YEAR	1992
TELEPHONE NUMBER	676—4211

ARITHMETIC calendar

Time seems to have such little meaning to some children. However, when a child makes his or her own calendar, in which the months are broken down into weeks and the weeks into days, the child begins to see "time" as something more tangible. The child begins to understand that weather conditions, seasons, holidays, and historical events come at special times within the calendar. As the days pass, each monthly calendar is saved, added to the others, and the whole given to the child at the end of the year.

Most of us use this little rhyme to recall the number of days in a month. A child would enjoy learning it too.

> Thirty days hath September
> April, June, and November
> All the rest have thirty-one
> Excepting February alone.
> And that has twenty-eight days clear.
> And twenty-nine in each leap year.

A calendar similar to this one is fun to make. See all the important information there is on it. And children can see it all at a glance.

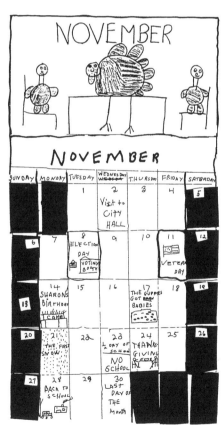

111

ARITHMETIC graphs

Children can learn to feel "at home" with graphs since graphs are basically "pictures of information."

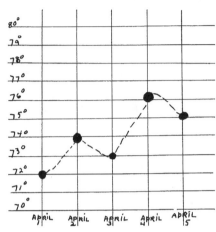

Graph of spelling tests for the week.

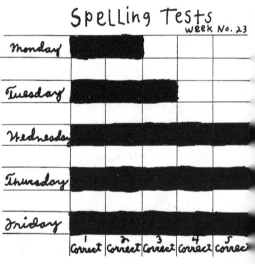

It's not always easy for some children to understand the meaning of "20% off," "5% raise," or "3% interest." A chart similar to this one can help a child "see" that 3% means three cents for every dollar.

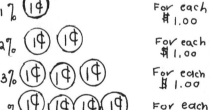

ARITHMETIC games

Have you ever come across a child who knows the leading baseball players and their averages or the child who can identify the various makes of cars? Yet, sometimes this very child may not be very good at math.

I have often wondered about this strange phenomenon and cannot help thinking there may be some truth to the expression, "Millions of twelve-cylinder brains hit on only one cylinder!" Perhaps *all* of us have more potential for learning than is actually used.

This is why games play such an important role for children. Children seem to get so involved that they forget their fears, inhibitions, or frustrations. Their interest and attention become intense; their bodies and minds seem to function at their highest abilities. (And thus we achieve a fertile situation for learning!)

Give a child a supply of wooden toothpicks and see how eagerly the child will want to make roman numerals. The child may learn all the numbers up to 12 (which is enough for reading the roman numerals on a clock). If the child is willing and adept, it will be fun to go all the way to 20 (which is more than enough for general use).

A set of dominoes is a great way to find "likenesses in numbers."

A quickly drawn stick figure or a few circles and lines can make the difference between a drill's becoming dull or fun!

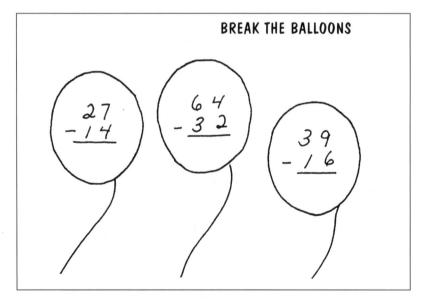

ARITHMETIC number notebook

Some children can pick up number concepts easily, but that doesn't make it any easier for those children who don't. A NUMBER NOTE-BOOK gives experience in associating a concrete amount with an abstract form.

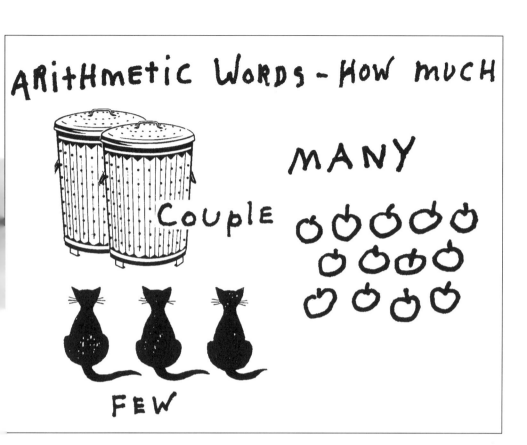

Common math-related concepts can be made more concrete by the use of appropriate pictures pasted into the notebook.

ARITHMETIC finger plays

Even older children sometimes enjoy FINGER PLAYS. There is hardly a young child who doesn't. Finger plays are useful in developing number concepts.

Try them using these traditional rhymes.

ONE FOR THE MONEY

One for the money *(Hold up one finger.)*
Two for the show *(Hold up two fingers.)*
Three to make ready *(Hold up three fingers.)*
Four to go. *(Hold up four fingers.)*

MOTHER HEN AND CHICKS

(Point to each finger to indicate the first, second, etc.)

Said the *first* little chicken with a queer little squirm,
"I wish I had a nice fat worm."

Said the *second* little chicken with an odd little shrug,
"I wish I could find a nice fat bug."

Said the *third* little chicken with a sigh of relief,
"I wish I could find a nice green leaf."

Said the *fourth* little chicken with a queer little squeal,
"I wish I could find some nice yellow meal."

"Now see here," said the mother hen from the green garden patch,

"If you want any breakfast, come here and scratch."

I LOVE SIXPENCE

(Hold up number of fingers as indicated.)

I love sixpence, pretty little sixpence,
I love sixpence better than my life;
I spent a penny of it, I spent another,
And took fourpence home to my wife.

Oh, my little fourpence, pretty little fourpence
I love fourpence better than my life;
I spent a penny of it, I spent another.
And I took twopence home to my wife.

Oh, my little twopence, my pretty little twopence,
I love twopence better than my life;
I spent a penny of it, I spent another
And took home nothing to my wife.

Oh, my little nothing, my pretty little nothing,
What will nothing buy for my wife?
I have nothing, I spent nothing,
I have nothing better than my wife.

FIVE LITTLE CHICKADEES

(Hold out five fingers, eliminating one gradually.)

Five little chickadees
Peeping at the door;
One flew away
And then there were four.

Four little chickadees
Sitting on a tree;
One flew away
And then there were three.

Three little chickadees
Looking at you;
One flew away
And then there were two.

Two little chickadees
Sitting in the sun;
One flew away
And then there was one.

One little chickadee
Left all alone;
One flew away
And then there were none.

117

ONE, TWO, BUCKLE MY SHOE

One, two, buckle my shoe
Three, four, shut the door
Five, six, pick up sticks
Seven, eight, make them straight
Nine, ten, a big fat hen.

ARITHMETIC other activities

A liking for numbers can start so early, much earlier than is commonly thought. Try these ideas and see.

1   Count the buttons on coat, shirt, blouse.
     Count the steps on the front porch, the back porch, how many steps there are leading upstairs, how many steps to the basement.
     Count the number of trees in front of your house, the neighbor's house, how many on the block, etc.
     Count the light poles you see on the way to the store.

2   What things come in two's? (shoes, socks, eyes—what else?)
     What things come in three's? four's?

3   A scrapbook with one picture of a ball and the numeral "1."
     Another with two like items and the numeral "2." Find them in looking over the newspaper together.

4   Print beginning numbers and let the child trace over and over them.

5   Can you make numbers on the ground with rope? or mud? or sand?

6   Do you see numbers that you recognize in the grocery store?

7   Look at house numbers when you go down the street. What is your house number? your neighbor's?

8   Play with a deck of cards and sort the same numbers together.

9   Matching.

10   Shuffleboard.

HOUSEHOLD FUN

7. HOUSEHOLD FUN

All children—boys and girls—should receive the same training in household tasks. (Perhaps if some of us adults had had this training when we went to school, some of us would be a little less helpless around the house!)

HOUSEHOLD FUN tasks

Do you ever wonder about what to do for a child and what *not* to do? It's not really easy to decide, because we as adults can usually do the work faster and better than a child.

Yet, if we don't give a child work responsibilities when young, we are really depriving the child. The negative results will eventually show up.

Many of these household jobs your child can perform willingly, reasonably well, and consistently:

    put toys away when finished playing with them
    empty the wastebaskets
    bring groceries in from the car
    sweep the sidewalk and driveway
    turn off lights when not needed
    bring in mail and newspaper
    feed household pets
    polish shoes
    dust the furniture
    help shovel snow
    clean some garden tools
    rake leaves
    water the garden
    separate laundry into whites, darks, etc.
    help hang and put away wash
    sweep the kitchen floor
    set the table
    bring dirty dishes to the sink
    wash and dry the dishes, and put them away

load and unload dishes if you have a dishwasher
dress and undress oneself independently
hang up all clothes properly
stack newspapers and magazines for recycling
bring baby's bottle and diaper when asked
answer the telephone properly
put on and take off seatbelt
change bedclothes and make bed

There are so many household tasks that children can learn to do:

They can learn to stop hinges from squeaking, fix doors and drawers that stick, and how to sharpen knives (including safety precautions).

OTHER HOUSEHOLD TASKS A CHILD CAN PERFORM ALONE OR ASSIST WITH:

❑ put on and take off storm and screen doors and windows
❑ locate a stud in the wall
❑ put up hooks for clothing
❑ put up shelves
❑ put up curtain rods and window shades
❑ hang a picture on a wall
❑ care for hardwood floors, vinyl floor coverings, etc.
❑ use and care for brooms, mops, and paintbrushes
❑ clean tubs and sinks
❑ care for upholstery
❑ clean off ice and snow in the winter
❑ care for garden tools
❑ separate the garbage and put recyclables where they belong
❑ take care of the garbage pails
❑ dust and polish the furniture
❑ polish silverware
❑ put outdoor toys away where they belong and leave play area neat
❑ hang out clothes to dry then put where they belong
❑ fill water and food dishes for pets.

When a child has pretty well mastered a job, by all means, he or she ought to assume the responsibility for doing it regularly.

HOUSEHOLD FUN electricity

The theoretical aspects of electricity can be beyond a child's ability to understand. However, some children can learn:

• How to change a fuse.

• How to turn off the electricity in case of emergency.

• How to use the toaster, iron, vacuum cleaner, and other appliances. And they must learn the safety precautions involved.

• How to change a light bulb and the different wattages of bulbs.

• What causes a short circuit.

Children can learn (by themselves) what gives off more light—a 100-watt bulb or a 40-watt bulb.

HOUSEHOLD FUN locks and keys

Wherever children are, there will always be locks or keys to use. Combination locks are not always easy to work—so a supply of them is good to practice on. (Sometimes a nearby locksmith can provide some to use.)

Bicycle locks,
for example, are important to
learn to use.

HOW TO OPEN A LOCK

1. Turn knob RIGHT - two or more times and —
2. Stop at 8
3. Turn knob LEFT one complete turn past 8 and stop at 31
4. Turn RIGHT to 44

HOUSEHOLD FUN sheet metal work

Older children may be able to learn how to use the soldering iron and pliers well enough to make some useful household items, such as

> pin trays
> bookends
> cookie cutters
> funnels
> dust pans.

Some children can learn to fix defective vases and certain pots and pans. It also gives them a chance to practice repairing loose handles—and some leaks too!

HOUSEHOLD FUN car cleaning

All of us know (only too well!) how disconcerting it is to take a car into a garage for repair only to find that the work was poorly done. Repair work on a car requires skill, and amateurs ought to be wary of trying to do this. But there are so many routine, uncomplicated jobs children and amateurs can do—and do well.

Either by watching or helping a parent—or even watching or helping at the nearby friendly gas station—children can perform several of these jobs rather well:

> how to help wash a car, including front, rear, and side windows
> how to help wax a car
> how to help grease some parts of the car
> how to help test air in the tires with a gauge
> how to help change a tire
> how to help an adult change the oil in the car

HOUSEHOLD FUN cooking

CARD FILE BOX

Some people are very well organized and have superb memories. Some minds are easily muddled and forgetful. Yet, because there is important information people must have at their fingertips, it is important to drill from day to day, week to week, month to month, and year to year.

There are, however, certain kinds of information that may just as well be recorded on a card and referred to as needed. For example, for some, it is hard to remember that there are 3 teaspoons in 1 tablespoon.

After many attempts to memorize this simple concept, a card is made and placed in the card file box. The child may refer to the card file many times. After a while the child has a full box of handy, easy-to-get-at information, ready to be looked up if necessary.

Some children may forget how to set the table from one meal to the next. To make sure they get it right every time, all that has to be done is to pluck the "table setting" card from the card file box and refer to it as needed.

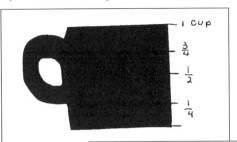

HOUSEHOLD FUN shopping for food

There is so much the shopper needs to know about foods:

What are the best apples for eating? for pies?

There are different kinds of potatoes. Which are best for boiling? for baking?

Is there a difference between white eggs and brown eggs? What are the different sizes of eggs?

How can you tell if bananas are ripe? a cantaloupe? a tomato? a peach?

Is there a quick test to see if the string beans are fresh?

What does fresh spinach look like? fresh carrots? lettuce?

Questions such as these can be answered if the children are taken on visits to the nearby grocer. Some store managers welcome visits by children, especially if the visits can be arranged during the "slow" time of the day.

HOUSEHOLD FUN cooking—social occasions

The art of hospitality does not come easily to most young people, and they can often be all "thumbs." Mother's Day is a good opportunity for practice. It gives children needed time to develop the background to help stage a social event gracefully.

There is nothing quite like a punch party to get children interested in learning the "ins and outs" of holding a successful social. There is a lot involved in planning for the refreshments, entertainment, type of clothing to wear, how to greet guests, cleaning up, and other details.

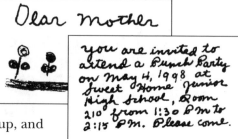

Dear mother

you are invited to attend a Punch Party on May 4, 1998 at Sweet Home Junior High School, Room 210 from 1:30 PM to 2:15 PM. Please come.

HOUSEHOLD FUN sewing

Simple sewing (such as the basting stitch) can be practiced on tagboard with yarn or colored thread. Beginning with large, oversized stitches, they are gradually made smaller until a normal size is reached.

Similar cards can be made for other basic stitches such as hemming, backstitch, overcast, and others. It's so easy and such fun to do—and at the same time, the child learns to do something that can be used throughout life.

HEMMING A SKIRT

Some years the "accepted" hemlines are very short and sometimes the "accepted" hemline is very long. Sometimes it's "middle-ish." Fashion designers change their ideas so often—almost from season to season. So it's very necessary for girls to learn to take up and let down hems.

Boys don't have this particular problem, but it wouldn't hurt one bit if boys *helped* their sisters or mother take up a hem or let down a hem for them!

BASTING STITCH

OVERCASTING STITCH

MADE-OVER CLOTHING

Many children have to wear "hand-me-downs." There should be no ill feelings about this at all—especially if the material is still in good condition and not faded. Children ought to learn to "make over" clothing.

With imagination . . .

> by turning the material,
> dyeing,
> or combining with other materials,
> cutting down a dress to make a blouse
>   or a skirt
> and dozens of other exciting tricks

Children can have wardrobes that become uniquely their own (and also get the precious satisfaction of being creative!).

Even if parents can afford to buy their children new clothing, by making clothing over we encourage the values of thrift and creative fun.

SEWING MACHINE

"Wait until you know how to sew by hand and then you can learn to use the sewing machine."

The sequence of learning to sew need not necessarily be important. It can be so discouraging to take hours to sew up a seam that could be "run up" by a sewing machine in minutes. What a sense of importance it gives the older child who can sew on the machine! And what fun it is!

Besides, the sooner children learn to use the machine, the more practice they will have doing the very thing that will be useful all their lives. So, if the child is mature enough, why not demonstrate the use of the machine at the same time the child is learning to sew by hand?

PATTERNS

It's lucky that there are special sewing-pattern books just with easy or very easy patterns. Even in regular pattern books there are sometimes special sections with easy patterns. Good! Another "plus" is the fact that many fashions are of the shapeless type, with no exact waistline, no intricate buttonholes to make, no form-fitting bustline, and so forth. How nice for children who are learning to sew!

Imagine making this lovely easy-to-make skirt in three different materials—one cotton, one corduroy, and another wool!

WRAP & TIE SKIRT

HOBBIES

How many children just sit and watch television "when they have nothing to do" (especially at night in many cases—hour after hour!). How many don't know anything else to do?

This is often a common complaint of parents, harder to take if the parents themselves are physically and intellectually active. But—among other activities—taking up handwork (like knitting, crocheting, and braiding) could be fulfilling, constructive, and turn out to be lots of fun.

First a child learns to "purl" and he or she can make a whole lovely scarf with just this one stitch.

Later on the child can learn to knit.

And then later on, combine the purl and the knit! (Scarves and sweaters are just two items children can make. And the satisfaction they get becomes priceless!)

Most children can "catch on" to braiding quite easily. And with one long braid, this same child can make a lovely rug by just (with a very easy stitch) sewing the braid together.

Hooked-rug making is another easy craft a child can learn because it involves just going "in and out" with the yarn and hook.

Embroidering a set of towels or napkins using a simple cross-stitch makes for a relaxing and useful pastime.

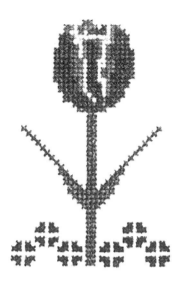

REPAIR WORK

Personally there is no household chore more distasteful to me (and perhaps for the reader too) than REPAIR WORK. Somehow, it seems that torn socks, the blouse with the ripped seam, and the stockings with a "run" find themselves in the dark recesses of the closet. There they wait (sometimes longer than I care to admit) until the proper mood or necessity strikes.

This is certainly not the attitude children should have. And so REPAIR WORK can become a kind of "special" occasion. Once every so often a child can have the "privilege" (!?) of just doing repair work. A big occasion is made of it—sitting down at a comfortable spot, serving some refreshments, chatting—and holding something like a quilting bee. In this setting, it's possible for the child to learn:

DARNING	Since the principle of darning is weaving, the children are first given weaving cards. Later, they may add the use of darning on white cloth and colored darning cotton.
PATCHING	The principle of patching can be made more clear if a paper patch is sewn over a paper hole, using colored thread.
BUTTON SEWING	It is not easy for some children to sew at a definite point. Buttons drawn on paper provide a way to practice putting a needle through a hole.

129

HOUSEHOLD FUN laundering

Do you remember the days when washday was called "Blue Monday"? I do. Washday was a day that was a real bother for any homemaker. How difficult it must have been carrying water in pails to the tubs for the washing and the rinsing, hanging out the clothes for drying, and ironing with a heavy hand-iron heated on the stove!

Nowadays (luckily) science has made it possible for most children to "do" the wash. For example:

- synthetic "wash-and-wear" clothing and "no-iron" fabrics that require a minimum amount of care
- automatic washers and dryers
- adjustable light-weight electric irons (with dials to adjust for cotton, wool, and other fabrics)
- a variety of special laundry aids (detergents, water softeners, bleaches, and sheets that remove static electricity)

Most children easily ought to be able to:

> empty pockets.
> close zippers.
> remove pins.
> roll down sleeves.
> separate the wash into colors.
> separate wash-and-wear clothes from others.

Once a child can learn to operate the "controls" on the automatic washing and drying machines, there is no reason why the child can't have the privilege (yes!) of doing the whole family wash alone.

With so many marvelous "no-iron" or "little ironing needed" fabrics, most children ought to be able to keep themselves in "tip-top" shape on their own.

If a child knows how to "set" the iron properly, whether it is for "wash-and-wear" shirts, a wool sweater, or handkerchiefs, looking neat "on his or her own" ought to be easy—and challenging too, at the same time!

HOUSEHOLD FUN child care

Ask most teenaged girls what they want to do most in life, and don't be surprised at their answer! Most want to get married and have children. And so, it is necessary to give teenagers opportunities to

> watch little children during their playing.
> teach little children easy games.

help little children put on and take off wraps, etc.

visit CHILD CARE CLINICS.

visit NURSERY SCHOOLS.

have visits to "infant sections" of local department stores.

drill, drill, drill on the handling, feeding, dressing, and bathing of little children.

Older children—when given an opportunity to take care of a baby—usually take their jobs very seriously. When giving the baby a bath, they know they must NEVER TAKE THEIR HANDS OFF THE BABY and NEVER LEAVE THE BABY ALONE. This means practicing to have everything ready for the bath (including everything that is necessary *before* the bath, *during* the bath, and *after* the bath).

Other ways for children to help (even younger children can learn to perform these jobs) include:

bringing diapers and bottles when needed

learning how a cranky baby will calm down when the carriage or bed is rocked—or how babies love to be taken for a little ride!

getting a cloth to wipe the baby (a younger child can do that too)

picking up something the baby throws to the floor and giving it back

How babies fuss and get irritable when handled too much! (But the use of tapes, adjustable snaps, and openings in the front and back of their little clothes can help the older child dress the infant more quickly and with a minimum of annoyance.

HOUSEHOLD FUN baby-sitting

Many older children enjoy baby-sitting. Perhaps this has something to do with a basic instinct nature has given the human being. In any case, many children seem to enjoy this responsibility. Even a younger child often enjoys being given a little of this important responsibility.

Having a responsibility for the care of babies involves:

learning to feed, clothe, and prepare them for bed

learning about such safety rules as keeping sharp objects away from babies

keeping the babies away from stairways, stoves, and other dangerous places and not to hurt a baby physically—ever!

Most important, the older child needs to know how to use the telephone properly in case of emergency.

131

HOUSEHOLD FUN other tasks

There is so much children can learn in order to make a contribution to family living. A concerted effort can help them to be useful and add to the closeness of the family—and so, to everyone's happiness.

With supervision they can learn:

1) to scrub carrots and potatoes, to use the peeler, how to cut them, etc.

2) to shell peas and snap string beans.

3) to sort washed and dried silverware—also to put silverware away properly.

4) to help put groceries away.

5) such tips as:

   what is the difference between cooking food in stainless steel ware and aluminum? ironwear? Are non-stick surfaces OK to use?

   how to return something to the store if it isn't right.

   what qualities to look for in buying bedsheets, towels, blankets.

   what makes a "good fit" in selecting a pair of trousers? a dress? a coat? sneakers?

   keeping receipts.

   saving and storing bags for recycling.

6) to use the vacuum cleaner or mop the kitchen floor.

7) to clean copper vases, pots, etc.

MUSIC

8. MUSIC

If you've tried hard to "reach" a child and are about to give up—do give music a chance.

It's hard to say why music works so well. Perhaps it's because music doesn't need words to "talk" to a child.

A fussy infant will drop off to sleep with a mother's lullaby.

A child may be gloomy and sullen, but the hypnotic power of music transforms the child into a galloping horse, a zooming airplane, or a dancing elf.

A frightened little boy forgets his fears, is drawn to the magnetic beat, and is impelled to shake his tambourine . . . softly at first . . . but a little while later . . . with complete abandon!

"No, I don't want to," another child balks. "Come, let's try" . . . "See, you have, and it was fun!" Just one stroke on an autoharp makes possible the precious feel of an immediate accomplishment.

When a stubborn girl jumps to her feet at the first chords of a march and demands, "Let me be first!"—then we know that music makes a difference.

The over-aggressive boy is calmed down (at least for a while) by the "Moonlight Sonata." He may let go later when he bangs on his drums.

When it's otherwise hard to "pay attention," children learn to do what the music "says." They play fast when the music tells them to play fast, play loud when the music says to, or stop when the music tells them to stop.

Children can get instant pleasure from music. There is no need to wait till tomorrow or next week for gratification!

MUSIC rhythm interpretation

If you're able to play the piano or any other instrument, that's good! If not, try using a record, a tape, some music on the radio or television set.

See how easily children will transform themselves into anything suggested. (However they respond, it's "their way" and we adults ought to accept it uncritically!)

Try some of these for rhythmic interpretations. Make believe you're

> a flower swaying in the wind
> birds flying in the sky
> a ballet dancer
> a farmer scattering the seeds about
> an orchestra director
> a mother pushing her child on a swing
> a skater

What else?

MUSIC playing instruments

Some may argue that "it doesn't pay to have a child learn to play an instrument . . . it takes too long and it's too hard . . . it's such a bother to get a child to practice . . . and besides, he'll never learn to play really well. . . ." There probably is some validity to some of these arguments.

I don't know though how we can possibly measure the feeling of satisfaction a child gets from accompanying others when they sing "Happy Birthday" at Mother's birthday party—or play a solo (even with the mistakes) for Grandma!

Any instrument just lying about (for example, an autoharp just resting on a table) can attract a child to feel like giving it a couple of plucks, and love to hear the sounds it makes. Who knows, someday this same child may want to learn to play it—or another instrument. At the very least, it can help (in however small a way) to develop a child's power to hear and enjoy beautiful sounds.

MUSIC square dancing

Anyone who has been to a square dance knows what fun it is—even if you do get mixed up "allemanding" to the right instead of "allemanding" to the left, lose your partner, or just have to flop on a chair in sheer exhaustion!

Children love to square dance too. If you don't know how to square dance, find someone who does. Experience has shown me that most square dancers are usually friendly, warm-hearted people who are eager to share their pleasures with others.

It wouldn't be too difficult to get some children together to have a square-dance group. For example, one "caller" gave up part of his Wednesdays (when his office was closed) to work with a group of children at a nearby school. Most children learned several dances in a short while and always had a great time! Incidentally, an invitation to a square-dance party is a wonderful way to make new children in the neighborhood feel "at home" and pleasantly comfortable quickly.

MUSIC popular dancing

I, and perhaps you, have had the humiliating experience of going to a party or a dance and being a "wallflower." Did you ever have this terrible feeling? In the course of time, though, most of us learned to dance reasonably well. What if you have a shy or somewhat withdrawn child? You don't want the child to grow up being a social misfit, always finding excuses to avoid social get-togethers.

Anything can justify a party—a birthday, a holiday, the first robin, or some new guinea-pig babies. Parties give children plenty of time to practice learning how to dance, plenty of time for those who are socially mature to teach others to learn to dance acceptably (and also enjoy it!).

MUSIC homemade instruments

It's interesting that most children seem to like to be in the kitchen more than in any other room in the house. Could it be that other rooms in the house have so many "don't touch!" things around?

In the kitchen, there is one special drawer for them—a drawer that they can go to with no "if's, and's, and but's." It's a special drawer full of marvelous:

> pots and pans
> metal spoons and wooden spoons
> jiggly measuring spoons

All of them are ready to use for an orchestra for dancing, for marches, or even just for listening to. Another special thing about this drawer is that things don't have to be put away neatly when you're done. You can just put them away "any old way"!

TAMBOURINE

1. Staple two paper plates
   together or lace them
   together with yarn.
2. Tie on small bells loosely.

BOTTLE XYLOPHONE

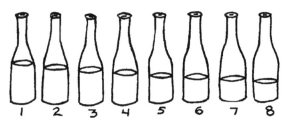

Use eight drinking glasses—or the children may prefer to use pop bottles brought from home. Fill with different amounts of water. Tune to piano notes by adding or pouring out water. Plink out the music with a pencil.

Three blind mice. Three blind mice.
  3   2   1   3   2   1

See how they run. See how they run.
5   4   4 3   5   4   4 3

They all ran af ter the farmer's wife
5   8 8 7 6 7   8   5   5

Who cut off their tails with a carving knife.
5   8   8 8   7   6   7 8 5   5

Did you ever see such a sight in your life as
5   8   8 8 7   6   7 8   5 5   5   4

Three blind mice.
  3   2   1

OTHER INSTRUMENTS TO MAKE

Pot Lid Cymbals — Dance away to the clang of two flat pot lids when they are banged together. Can you make loud and soft sounds?

Tin Can Rattle — Put some pennies or bottlecaps inside an empty tin can and roll it around the floor. Listen to the different sounds that are made.

Drum or Tom-Tom — Any one of these things would make a fine drum for any marching band. Listen and you will hear that each of them makes a different sound. Ask the children which they would choose:

> a kitchen pot or pan?
> a metal or plastic pail?
> a plastic bleach bottle?
> any big can—like a coffee or paint can?
> an empty oatmeal box?

Chimes — If you get a stick or ruler—and dangle a knife, a fork, and a teaspoon from it, then tap it with a spoon—you can have a glorious set of chimes.

Hub Cap Gong — Suspend a hub cap in the air and strike it with a stick.

Spoon Bells — Suspend spoons from a coat hanger. Strike with another spoon.

Potato Grater — If you have a potato grater, you can get four different sounds, one from each side of the grater.

Rattles — Some dried beans or pebbles in a tin can will make an elegant rattle. Or try bottle caps on a string.

Rhythm Sticks — When you tap two sticks together, you have a set of rhythm sticks. (Of course, if you attach ribbon streamers to them, they become very special.)

Tambourine — String small bells together and lace them through the edges of a stiff paper plate. Then shake it or tap it on your knee.

MUSIC bands

Don't think of what they do to the music, but what the music is doing for them!

When you stop to think about it, belonging to a funny little band does a great deal for the children. They organize it. They make all the instruments. They give the band its name. They have their own conductor. They call their own rehearsals. They select their own songs to play.

But—most important of all—is the training they get from working together. They begin to feel that the group could not function completely without their cooperation. They begin to feel "needed"—a feeling so important for good mental health. They can play in their homes or yards, serenade at birthday parties, become marching bands going down the street, and present concerts from time to time for the neighborhood.

MUSIC orchestra instruments

Wooden sticks tapped on the desk or on metal, or plucking strings and rubber bands—all have special sounds of their own. The child's fascination with this phenomenon can lead to the study of the instruments of the orchestra. It isn't that we expect the child to learn to play these instruments, for (though we are always hopeful) we always try to be realistic. It is only that we want to encourage the child's power to hear.

MUSIC school orchestra

As long as children do not have to worry about "who composed what," "key," "mood," "theme," and other technical matters, they can just sit back and watch any amateur group rehearse.

Most groups would welcome an audience during rehearsals (school groups, neighborhood groups—sometimes even professional groups). But, of course, you have to be quiet.

Children can see how an orchestra works, the various kinds of instruments, the work of the conductor, and so forth. Most important of all for any child to see is teamwork in action (and this provides valuable lessons to think about!).

With successive listening, the ears become attuned to music and the emotional pleasure it offers. You can see this easily in children's reaction to the trumpets blaring away in the Grand March of *Aida* or the tapping to the steady beat of Schubert's *March Militaire*.

MUSIC talent shows

On a rainy afternoon when three or four friends get together, a music-and-dance Talent Show is lots of fun. And children love to dress up and be someone else. Anything can inspire a dance:

> a cowboy hat
> a scarf
> a worn sheet
> a leaf
> even a feather.

The performer can always expect lots of applause and appreciation from the audience.

It's always interesting to watch how—even in a family—an aggressive child will seize the opportunity to be in the limelight, while "retiring" ones automatically form the audience (not for long, however, for the latter are gradually drawn into participation).

MUSIC chorus

If there is an activity that just about every child can participate in with some success, it's a chorus. Most choruses have a few strong singers, those most able to lead the group. The others are usually followers who sing along as best they can. (If the followers don't sing too loudly, no one will hear their mistakes. Besides, the benefits to the followers far outweigh any of their musical shortcomings. Each child is enriched by being with others as they have fun and sing along together.)

MUSIC listening opportunities

Do you have any friends who are amateur or professional musicians? Ask them if your child might listen to them practice. (Most musicians like an audience and you'll see how eagerly most will answer, "Of course.")

One friend (a member of a local Philharmonic Orchestra) enjoys her violin so much, she plays for anyone who will listen. Another friend loves to sing and has a delightful selection of Viennese songs she translates for her audiences. A flutist friend is fun too—especially if he brings along his birdlike piccolo!

Our daughter, Paula, will play her guitar for children wherever she can. Not only will she play, but joyfully leads whatever audience she has (big or little, young or old). She plays everyone's favorites. Paula also loves to lead her audiences in singing.

There are lots of Paulas all over who would be happy to share their music. These are some of Paula's favorites for children:

Hush, Little Baby
She'll Be Coming 'Round the Mountain
Jacob's Ladder
Hole in the Bucket
This Old Man
My Darling Clementine
Frere Jacques (Brother John)
Down in the Valley
Blue Tail Fly
Big Rock Candy Mountain
There Was an Old Woman
Kum Ba Yah
Green Grass Grows All Around

MUSIC miscellaneous music classics

Children hear rock, jazz, country, and blues music often. But on a rainy day when two or three friends are together, they just may care to listen to some classical music. Yes! (Don't underestimate the power of the classics to attract young listeners, classics that have stood the test of time.) Selections that are unusually rhythmical "hold" children's attention, and most children respond naturally to them.

The Swan	Saint-Saens
Blue Danube Waltz	Strauss
Minute Waltz	Chopin

Lots of children feel "at home" with the popular hits they see and hear in classic movies, such as:

My Fair Lady   *South Pacific*   *Mary Poppins*

Program music is made to order for children since they can listen to the music as it goes along with the story. Some favorites include:

The Sorcerer's Apprentice	Dukas
Peter and the Wolf	Prokofiev
Nutcracker Suite	Tchaikovsky
Peer Gynt	Grieg

142

MUSIC rounds

Children can sing ROUNDS with friends. Rounds are such fun. You don't need a piano or an instrument to accompany you.

A round can be sung anywhere—

> at school
> at home
> on a walk
> in the car
> around a campfire.

Children don't have to worry about being shy or that they don't have the greatest voice in the world. (No wonder just about everyone in the world loves to sing rounds.) Try this one:

> Row, row, row your boat
> Gently down the stream.
> Merrily, merrily, merrily, merrily
> Life is but a dream.

When you get to the first "merrily," the second person starts singing the song too. Both of you continue singing the song three times or as many times as you like.

Now try these rounds:

OH, HOW LOVELY IS THE EVENING

> Oh, how lovely is the evening
> Is the evening
> When the bells are sweetly ringing, sweetly ringing
> Ding, dong, ding, dong, ding, dong.

SOFTLY SINGS THE DONKEY

> Softly sings the donkey
> At the break of day
> If you do not feed him
> You will have to hear him say,
> Hee-Haw! Hee-Haw! Hee-Haw! Hee-Haw! Hee-Haw!
> Hee-Haw! Hee-Haw! Hee-Haw! Hee-Haw! Hee-Haw!

ARE YOU SLEEPING

Are you sleeping,
Are you sleeping,
Brother John, Brother John?
Morning bells are ringing,
Morning bells are ringing,
Ding, ding, dong. Ding, ding, dong.

GOOSE ROUND

Why shouldn't my goose
Sing as well as their goose,
When I paid for my goose,
Twice as much as thine?

LITTLE TOM TINKER

Little Tom Tinker got burned by a clinker
And he began to cry,
"Ma-Ma!—What a poor fellow am I!"

MUSIC miscellaneous sounds

There are so many other opportunities to hear music. Children can listen to:

1) the birds when taking a walk
2) the wind as it blows through the trees
3) band concerts in the park
4) a symphony concert at the lakeshore
5) a college marching band
6) a barbershop quartet
7) hymns sung at religious services.

A child can even listen to the sound of an eggbeater whirling
      or
strike two wooden spoons together to make music to enjoy.

9. ART

Copying pictures, "painting by number," following dots, pouring plaster into ready-made molds, pre-cut craft kits—in none of these activities are children given the opportunity to express themselves freely. (I have often wondered how much potential creativity has been allowed to wither away by disuse in such unimaginative projects.)

It is often said that most children are not creative. I think they are. Every child is different from another.

> Families are different.
> Families live in different environments.
> Each child has had different experiences in life.

When these differences are knit together, each child becomes a distinctive person with a distinctive set of values and responses.

IT IS THIS DISTINCTIVENESS FROM WHICH WE CAN PULL
THE RAW MATERIALS FOR CREATIVITY.

> "Please don't correct me. . . .
> Let me draw the way I feel. . . .
> Let me pretend. . . .
> I know you want to help me. . . .
> But just as soon as you want me to do it your way
> I begin to feel
> It's no use trying and I begin to feel bad about myself."

Different materials, activities, and projects give a child the chance to experiment and explore.

You can "draw" just about anything you want by tearing paper into shapes.

This is John's calendar. Doesn't John's APRIL have a tender charm that touches the heart? Why not make a calendar too?

A COLLAGE is a fun way to introduce geometric shapes to children. Can you "draw" something else with these shapes?

148

See the difference between drawing a person WITHOUT LOOKING at him or her. Now draw the person by LOOKING at the person. You can see a lot more by looking and keeping your eyes wide open, can't you?

This sensitive drawing came after a field trip to our local art gallery, where there was a Van Gogh exhibit.

CHERRY ORCHARD
Vincent Van Gogh loved Nature. He loved trees. He loved trees in the spring.

This is Charles' family, his father, mother, his brother, and Charles. "Honey" (his dog) isn't here because "she's sleeping." Notice the sky and the earth. This is the way Charles sees the world. It isn't fair to make him try to see it our way.

This expressive drawing of being caught in the rain came after preliminary discussion of questions such as:

Do you like the rain?
What does rain make you want to do?
How do you feel when you hear thunder?
    when it grows dark?

When Mary starts to think about these questions, she begins (in her own way) to think creatively. And her results show this.

I have always wondered why so many children like BLOCK PRINTING.
    Do they get the same good
        feeling that
            comes from whittling a
            twig?
    I wonder . . .
        or are they drawn to the
        priceless bit of suspense
        that comes when the
        inked block is finally lifted?

Nature gives us endless examples of beauty to enjoy (grass, trees, flowers, birds, etc.). PEOPLE make things of beauty too, like a handmade sweater, the webbing of a tennis racquet, the colors of the cars in the parking lot.

A notebook with the theme "BEAUTY IS ALL AROUND" can help children to become aware of the beauty all around us.

150

WE ALL WORK TOGETHER

It must be admitted that there was some very loud discussion before, during, and after this mural was made by this group of children. But as important as the mural itself was the priceless experience of working together. Learning to work together—cooperation—comes best by "doing" and "practicing." Talking about cooperation alone will not suffice.

This is a page from a book made after a field trip to the Fairmont Milk Company.

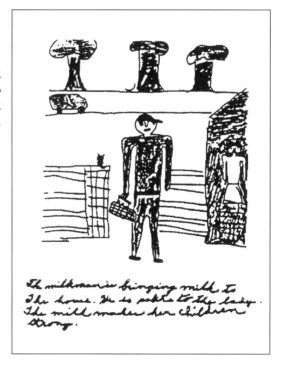

PAPER

Isn't it fun just to scribble—with no one to tell you to make this or that?

Scribbling can be done anywhere. Children can scribble

> on paper on the floor
> on paper on the table
> on old newspapers
> on the blackboard
> on used wrapping paper
> on paper dishes
> on the sidewalk.

Can you get hold of some old wallpaper books? Those are great for scribbling on too.

If you want someone to admire the children's masterpieces, do you have a bulletin board in your house? Or why not pin them to a string suspended across the room? You can hang them on a clothes hanger with clothespins too.

If you have some leftover paper, it's tons of fun just to rip and tear it. It makes a great ZZZZZ sound.

Also, you can punch holes in the paper with a wooden spoon.

CARDBOARD

How about making puzzles from cardboard? (Puzzles are fun to make and put together. And they don't cost any money either.)

They're so easy to make too. Ask the children to pick out a picture from an old newspaper or magazine and mount it on the cardboard with glue.

Then ask them to cut the picture into one, two, three, or more pieces. (Be sure to put the pieces in a bag so that they don't get lost.)

Can they reassemble the picture puzzle? Do they have a little sister or brother who would like to try?

CLAY

There are so many wonderful things children can make with clay. Anything in the whole world can be made from clay. Children can make a house, a castle, a snowman, a dog, an apple—anything!

And the best part is, they can

> poke it hard
> push it in or out
> pat it gently or hard
> roll it over and over and over
> punch it
> squeeze it
> and make it so nice and smooth.

You don't always have to buy clay. Why not go over to that new construction site. There might be some clay the workers would let you have. I am sure they will say OK, so be sure to bring along a bag to put some of the clay in.

Of course, there might be a clay spot right in the students' own gardens that Mom or Dad or caretaker would let them have. (Think of all the delicious pies and cakes that children could make!)

SOME OTHER ART ACTIVITIES TO TRY

Make a SILHOUETTE PICTURE of a brother's, sister's, or a friend's body. Here's what to do.

> Place a big sheet of paper on the floor.
> Have the person lie on the paper.
> Trace the body.
> Paint the silhouette black.
> Cut out the silhouette.
> Paste it on a large sheet of paper.
> Then hand it up for everyone to enjoy.

When the person lies on the paper, he or she can get into all kinds of positions for tracing.

Do you have a large three-way **MIRROR?** Ask the children to draw themselves from the different angles.

ROPE is not just good for "playing rope" with friends. Ask the students if they have ever tried drawing pictures with rope—or numbers, or letters of the alphabet.

A whole pile of **BUTTONS** in different sizes and in different colors is very good for "drawing" different pictures. Children can "draw" people, houses, trees—anything! (You can "draw" with bottle tops too!)

Did you ever think that **BRICKS** could be good for anything besides building houses? Bricks have a great rough texture and lovely pictures can be painted on them. (If it's an especially good picture, perhaps it can be used as a doorstop. You can even use them for bookends if you have two of them.)

SAND is very good for making castles, houses, and cakes—but also for making pretty pictures by tracing a finger through it!

SUMMARY

Courses in the field of Special Education and General Education can teach only the basic principles for working with children. None can give pat, reliable methods for achieving a particular result.

Yet, I feel sure that each teacher and each parent has enough creativity, using tools like the activities presented here, to come up with solutions for particular needs. As you work with children day in and day out, you will have many opportunities to develop this creativity. I feel sure that as you search and experiment, you will discover within yourself undreamed-of talents. You will discover the secret formula for creating the necessary bond to reach each child according to his or her individual needs.

In this creative process, you will grow. And so too will your children, who, learning by doing, look to you to show them how, not just to survive, but to live a *meaningful* life.

NOTES